With confetti falling and
surrounded by ESPN cameras,
head coach Urban Meyer
and his team celebrate their
national championship.
(Adam Cairns/Dispatch)

This book is book is available in quantity at special discounts for your group or organization. For further information, contact:

Triumph Books LLC
814 North Franklin Street
Chicago, Illinois 60610
Phone: (312) 337-0747
www.triumphbooks.com

Printed in U.S.A.
ISBN: 978-1-62937-057-6

The Columbus Dispatch
John F. Wolfe, Chairman & Publisher
Michael J. Fiorile, President & CEO
Benjamin J. Marrison, Editor
Philip Pikelny, Vice President & Chief Marketing Officer
Staff: Tim May, Bill Rabinowitz, Kyle Robertson, Adam Cairns, Eamon Queeney, Jonathan Quilter, Fred Squillante, Barbara J. Perenic, Jenna Watson, Brooke LaValley, Chris Russell, Ray Stein, Linda Deitch, Craig Holman, Karl Kuntz and Kirk Arnott

Content packaged by Mojo Media, Inc.
Joe Funk: Editor
Jason Hinman: Creative Director

Front and back cover photos by Adam Cairns/Dispatch.

CONTENTS

INTRODUCTION

By Ben Marrison

Tim May has witnessed plenty of Ohio State football. The *Dispatch* reporter's perspective on the Buckeyes' improbable and unexpected national championship speaks volumes about the 2014 team's storybook season.

"This is the greatest national championship in Ohio State history, in my opinion. I have covered 31 straight seasons, and just the challenge of replacing two quarterbacks and persevering made this a season to remember," May said. "But more than that, the Buckeyes had to do something no other team in college football history had ever done: win two postseason games to earn the first College Football Playoff championship."

Bill Rabinowitz, who covers Ohio State football alongside May for *The Dispatch*, puts this team in a special place in history as well. "I doubt that there's ever been a national championship team quite like this one," he said. "Has any team — college or pro — ever won a championship never using its expected starting quarterback, using its second-string quarterback most of the season and its third-string quarterback for the playoffs? I doubt it."

If you go back to the preseason, many (except perhaps ESPN's Mark May) considered the Buckeyes a national title contender. They were young and inexperienced in many positions, but were returning a front-runner for the Heisman Trophy in quarterback Braxton Miller. Another strong recruiting class had added speed and depth to a team that needed them. Coach Urban Meyer had brought in co-defensive coordinator Chris Ash to help stiffen a defense that was exposed during the final two

games of the 2013 season. They were playing in the Big Ten, a conference that was perceived to be weak, allowing them a less-than-challenging path to the national championship game in Arlington, Texas.

The Buckeyes were ranked fifth in the AP preseason poll and seventh in the *USA TODAY* poll. But before the ball was placed on the tee for the opener in Baltimore's M&T Bank Stadium, their season would be turned on its head.

Miller reinjured his right shoulder, the throwing arm he had so severely injured in the Orange Bowl against Clemson in January and would need surgery again. The season seemed lost.

"That August night when I got a call from a good source that I needed to check on Braxton, I thought it was a joke," May recalled. "We'd just talked to Miller at lunchtime. I'd written a story for the next day that the time had come finally for him to crank it up in preseason practice. Instead, as the story I broke revealed, he had suffered a season-snuffing dislocation of his right shoulder that included a tear of the labrum. That was stunning."

A spirited competition in the closing weeks of training camp left redshirt freshman J.T. Barrett as the starter, leaping over sophomore Cardale Jones — the guy most people assumed would be the next man up behind Miller.

After a sluggish victory over Navy in Baltimore, the Buckeyes slipped to eighth in the AP poll. They didn't look like national championship contenders.

The next game would be a defining one. In its home opener, Ohio State's youth was exposed: The offensive line, which returned just one starter, was

Alongside his wife, Shelley, head coach Urban Meyer hoists the championship trophy following his team's victory against Oregon. (Adam Cairns/Dispatch)

overmatched by the blitzing Virginia Tech defense, and Barrett was hammered repeatedly. He played like a quarterback making his second start. The loss to the unranked Hokies dropped the Buckeyes from the national championship conversation.

While some point to the loss as the galvanizing moment for this Buckeyes team, others pointed to the Oct. 25 game in Happy Valley against Penn State.

"After that double-overtime win at Penn State, a game that turned out to be tougher than most had expected, defensive end Joey Bosa said an interesting thing," May recalled. "He said there was a true sense of team as the Buckeyes found a way to rescue the night and the season in one of the more intimidating venues in college football. Looking back, I have to say he was right."

It was Bosa who made the game-winning, game-ending play by overpowering the Nittany Lions' offensive line to sack quarterback Christian Hackenberg in double overtime.

The dramatic win should have given the team a boost nationally. But critics kept pointing to the Virginia Tech loss.

"The loss to Virginia Tech hung from Ohio State's neck like an albatross for almost two months," May said, "but then came the upset win at Michigan State and suddenly the Buckeyes were being taken seriously again."

After that 49-37 win, the Buckeyes earned some respect: Ohio State jumped to eighth in the College Football Playoff and AP rankings. But sloppy play against Minnesota and Indiana let the doubters continue to question whether Meyer's team was worthy of football's final four.

The week before the rivalry game against Michigan, a tight-knit team became even more unified. Defensive lineman Kosta Karageorge left his apartment early one morning and couldn't be found. The Buckeyes wore Karageorge's number, 53, on their helmets. When the seniors were introduced at Ohio Stadium before the game, the 104,000-plus waited for Karageorge to miraculously walk onto the field. It didn't happen.

The game played out in familiar fashion, with Ohio State leading — but not comfortably. Then disaster struck: J.T. Barrett was tackled and went down awkwardly. He lay on the field, the stadium hushed. His ankle was broken.

The next man up was Jones. As he finished the Michigan victory, the questions were just beginning: Could Ohio State win it all with a third-string quarterback?

Days later, Karageorge's body was found in a trash bin not far from his apartment. He had committed suicide. The news devastated the team yet steeled it at the same time — just in time for the Big Ten championship game against Wisconsin.

Entering the game as a four-point underdog, Ohio State played like a team possessed. It was nearly perfect, routing Wisconsin 59-0 and shutting down its Heisman-finalist running back, Melvin Gordon. Jones, making his first college start, stunned the football world with his incredible arm strength and unexpected poise, earning the game's MVP award.

The resounding victory, coupled with the stellar play of Jones, hushed most of Ohio State's critics and propelled the Buckeyes into football's final four.

Their prize? Alabama. The oddsmakers had the Crimson Tide favored by nine points in the Sugar Bowl. Once again, the Buckeyes faced a Heisman finalist — this time in receiver Amari Cooper. After falling behind early, Ohio State rallied behind the rushing of unassuming Ezekiel Elliott and the passing game led by Jones. Cooper was not a factor.

And then the Buckeyes faced the Oregon Ducks and Heisman winner Marcus Mariota for the College Football Playoff championship in Arlington, Texas. Once again, Ohio State was the underdog.

The Buckeyes got off to a poor start, with Oregon taking a 7-0 lead on the opening possession. After that, the defense rose up and stuffed the Ducks most of the game. Sloppy play on offense — the Buckeyes committed four turnovers — kept Oregon in the game into the second half, but a resilient defense kept the Ducks from taking the lead.

Ohio State played a very physical game and was determined to win. The defensive line shut down Mariota by keeping the pressure on him all game. He didn't play like the nation's best player when faced with that defensive pressure.

On the other side of the ball, the young offensive line that played so poorly against Virginia Tech played like veterans, pushing the Ducks around to open holes

for Elliott. The sophomore running back was a beast, torching Oregon for 246 yards and four touchdowns. Elliott fought for every inch, and turned those inches into yards — and touchdowns.

Rabinowitz, who has studied Ohio State football history and written some of it, spelled out this team's special place in it.

"Even beyond the J.T. Barrett/Cardale Jones stories, this was a Buckeye team that evoked the magical 'Super Sophs' 1968 title team. So many of the key players were freshmen and sophomores that even Urban Meyer figured that a national title run was a year away," Rabinowitz said.

"But the Virginia Tech defeat galvanized them. Instead of wilting after that dispiriting loss, it made them rededicate themselves. An overhauled offensive line developed quickly under coach Ed Warinner. Ezekiel Elliott, playing essentially with one arm because

his left wrist was fractured in training camp, seemed to improve every week, as did a receivers group that embraced blocking as much as catching passes.

"The defense, with some hiccups along the way, finally found its identity. Defensive end Joey Bosa became an All-America player, and tackle Michael Bennett played at that level late. The improvement of the linebackers, from the out-of-nowhere Darron Lee to the finally-he-matured Curtis Grant, was instrumental."

Improvement came across the board. "But most of all, the success came from a coaching staff led by Urban Meyer that demanded excellence and, more important, painstakingly showed players how to achieve it," Rabinowitz said. "Despite their youth, despite the injuries, this Buckeyes team never lost faith in itself. Now it goes down as one of the storied teams in a storied program's history." ■

The triumphant Buckeyes, who overcame adversity and injury during their championship campaign, pose on the field of AT&T Stadium. (Kyle Robertson/Dispatch)

SUGAR BOWL

OHIO STATE 42, ALABAMA 35
January 1, 2015 • New Orleans, Louisiana

ROLLING OVER THE TIDE

Elliott Rushes for 230 Yards as OSU Rallies Back From 21-6 Deficit

By Bill Rabinowitz

In the victorious locker room, Ohio State players wore T-shirts that read "WON NOT DONE."

Tyvis Powell clutched the football that he intercepted to clinch the Buckeyes' gripping 42-35 Sugar Bowl victory over top-ranked Alabama in the College Football Playoff semifinals.

Michael Bennett and Adolphus Washington consented to an interview only if they did it together, such is their bond in the middle of the Ohio State defensive line.

Such is the bond among the entire team, and how necessary it's been for a team that has become the embodiment of resilience.

A team that has lost two star quarterbacks this season, that fell behind 21-6 to the pre-eminent program in college football, that made the ending heart-wrenching after it seemingly had the game in hand, is now a victory over Oregon away from winning the national championship.

The Buckeyes (13-1) will play the Ducks on Jan. 12 in suburban Dallas. Ohio State will be underdogs again. They will not care a whit.

On a day when the Big Ten reasserted its strength with stirring victories by Michigan State and Wisconsin in premier games, Ohio State came through with the biggest.

"That was a sledgehammer game," Buckeyes coach Urban Meyer said. "That was a classic."

No one would disagree.

It was a game that had almost everything. Momentum shifts that left one team staggering and then the other. Record-breaking performances. A razzle-dazzle touchdown by Ohio State. Even the punters — Ohio State's Cameron Johnston and Alabama's JK Scott — were worth the hefty price of admission.

The Buckeyes dominated the game statistically in the first half but were thwarted by two turnovers and the inability to score touchdowns twice when they had first-and-goal near the Alabama goal line.

When Alabama converted those turnovers into touchdowns and added another on its one sustained drive of the first half to take a 15-point lead, the Buckeyes looked on the verge of being knocked out.

Instead, Ohio State showed the resolve it has had all year. The Buckeyes scored two touchdowns in the final three minutes of the first half. The first came on a 3-yard run by Ezekiel Elliott, who broke the Sugar

Cardale Jones, who had 43 rushing yards during the Sugar Bowl, hurdles Alabama defensive backs Geno Smith (24) and Nick Perry (27). (Adam Cairns/Dispatch)

"THAT WAS A SLEDGEHAMMER GAME. THAT WAS A CLASSIC."
— URBAN MEYER

Running back Ezekiel Elliott elevates over Alabama safety Landon Collins (26) during his 54-yard, first-quarter run, which set the tone for the Sugar Bowl. (Eamon Queeney/Dispatch)

Bowl rushing record with 230 yards against a defense that had yielded only 88 yards a game on the ground this season.

"(Hall of Fame running back) Barry Sanders said before the game there were two great running backs that were going to play tonight, and they both were for 'Bama," Elliott said. "I felt a little bit left out."

The second TD came on some trickery. Jalin Marshall took the handoff from quarterback Cardale Jones and gave it to Evan Spencer. The wide receiver then threw to tightly covered Michael Thomas, who leaped and barely kept his foot inbounds for a touchdown with 12 seconds left in the half.

The Buckeyes continued their momentum to start the second half. Jones, who had been shaky early in his second career start, connected on a 47-yard touchdown pass to Devin Smith to put Ohio State ahead for the first time since it led 3-0.

Then defensive end Steve Miller made the biggest defensive play of the game. He dropped back in coverage, read the eyes of Alabama quarterback Blake Sims, made the easy interception and returned it 41 yards for a touchdown.

But Alabama hasn't been the country's dominant team in recent years for no reason. Derrick Henry caught a middle screen and ran for a 52-yard score. Four plays later, Sims ran for a 5-yard touchdown.

Ohio State's offense, saddled by terrible field position all game because of Scott's punts, had done little since early in the third quarter. When the Buckeyes got the ball with four minutes left, they were in desperate need of a big play. They got it. Elliott found a hole opened by blocks from Spencer and left guard Billy Price and ran for an 85-yard touchdown.

Wide receiver Michael Thomas catches a 13-yard touchdown pass from wide receiver Evan Spencer on a trick play right before halftime. (Jonathan Quilter/Dispatch)

"THIS IS ONE OF THE GREAT TEAM WINS WE'VE BEEN A PART OF."
— URBAN MEYER

After his 40-yard reception, wide receiver Devin Smith just barely missed out on scoring a touchdown during the first quarter. (Eamon Queeney/Dispatch)

Up 14 with 3:24 left after Smith caught a two-point conversion pass, the Buckeyes should have felt secure.

Nope.

Alabama needed only 77 seconds to score with star receiver Amari Cooper catching his second touchdown pass of the game.

When Spencer recovered the onside kick, Ohio State should have felt secure with Alabama having only two timeouts.

Nope.

Meyer called for a deep pass to Spencer that fell incomplete.

"It was my call to throw it down the field," Meyer said, explaining that Alabama stacked the line and was vulnerable deep. "Maybe it wasn't the right call. So I just kept thinking I screwed this up."

The Buckeyes punted, giving Alabama one last chance. The Crimson Tide moved the ball to the OSU 42 with 8 seconds left. Sims threw a Hail Mary into the end zone, and Powell intercepted the pass to clinch it.

"You have to congratulate Ohio State, who played a really, really good game, and we probably didn't play our best game," said Alabama coach Nick Saban.

Meyer wouldn't necessarily agree with that assessment.

"This is one of the great team wins we've been a part of," he said, "because we didn't play well at times but found a way to win." ■

Running back Ezekiel Elliott effectively seals the Ohio State victory with his 85-yard touchdown run with just 3:24 left in the Sugar Bowl. (Adam Cairns/Dispatch)

COLLEGE FOOTBALL PLAYOFF NATIONAL CHAMPIONSHIP

OHIO STATE 42, OREGON 20
January 12, 2015 • Arlington, Texas

PLAYOFF PAYOFF!

Elliott Runs for Four Touchdowns; Defense Answers Challenge

By Bill Rabinowitz

Say it slowly and let it sink in. It really happened. You aren't dreaming.

The Ohio State Buckeyes, counted out so many times this season, are the kings of college football.

This resilient 2014 team, a combination of 1968 youth and 2002 grit, overcame four turnovers to roll over Oregon 42-20 in the championship game of the inaugural College Football Playoff at AT&T Stadium.

Counted out after losing Braxton Miller before the season and falling to Virginia Tech in their second game, the Buckeyes (14-1) won their sixth national championship in school history in front of a mostly Ohio State crowd of 85,609.

The national title is the third for Urban Meyer, who won two at Florida and now has brought one to his home state.

"We finished the year a great team," Meyer said. "To have four turnovers and still beat a team like that 42-20, incredible experience. I don't want to get overdramatic, but it's as improved a football team (as I've seen) — and I've watched for a long time — from Game 1 to Game 15. I've never seen anything like it."

Sophomore Ezekiel Elliott continued his stunning late-season run by weaving and powering for 246 yards and four touchdowns behind an offensive line that punished Oregon to earn MVP honors.

"A monster," Meyer said.

One-time third-string quarterback Cardale Jones was nearly flawless, throwing for 242 yards and a touchdown and repeatedly using his 6-foot-5, 250-pound frame to bull for key first downs.

The defense, which many expected to wilt under the pressure of stopping Heisman Trophy winner Marcus Mariota's orchestration of Oregon's turbo-paced offense, was stout after a bad start. The 20 points were the fewest the Ducks scored all season.

"We just had to settle down and adjust to their tempo," co-defensive coordinator Chris Ash said. "You can't simulate that in practice."

Ohio State led 21-10 at halftime, but that lead was threatened when the turnover bug that began in the first half flared up again. Oregon (13-2) intercepted a pass that glanced off Jalin Marshall. On the next play, Mariota threw deep to Byron Marshall, who was wide open for a 70-yard touchdown.

Oregon looked poised to regain the lead when Jones fumbled while starting to throw under duress and lost the ball at the Buckeyes' 23. Oregon got it to the 6 before Eli Apple prevented a touchdown catch by Evan Baylis by pushing the tight end out of the end zone before he could get his feet down. Oregon's field goal made it 21-20.

That was as close as the Ducks would get as Elliott and the offensive line took over. The Buckeyes

Running back Ezekiel Elliott rushes for a 33-yard touchdown, the first of his four on the night. (Adam Cairns/Dispatch)

Ohio State made headlines with its impressive national championship victory against Oregon. (Eamon Queeney/Dispatch)

answered with a 12-play, 75-yard drive with Elliott doing most of the heavy lifting, finally scoring on a 9-yard carry.

Ohio State made it 35-20 with just under 10 minutes left on a similar drive, and Ohio State's defense prevented Mariota from providing any late magic.

"We knew that our O-line was bigger and more physical than their D-line," Elliott said, "and we just had to punch them in the mouth. They played their butts off, and they paved the way for me."

Ohio State led 21-10 at halftime after 30 minutes in which both teams had reason to wonder what-if.

The Buckeyes didn't even force Oregon into facing third down on the game's opening possession, a 75-yard touchdown drive. But then the Ducks dropped third-down passes on their next two possessions. On the second, Dwayne Stanford was alone behind the Buckeyes' defense.

After a slow start, Ohio State's offense started rolling. Elliott weaved for a 33-yard touchdown to cap a 97-yard drive to tie the score. Then his thumping 17-yard run set up Nick Vannett's 1-yard touchdown catch to put the Buckeyes ahead 14-7.

But it could have been a bigger margin. Two turnovers — a botched exchange between Jones and Elliott and a fumble by Corey Smith after a 50-yard reception — kept the Buckeyes from completely seizing control. The Smith fumble came after a goal-line stand by Ohio State's defense.

The Buckeyes made it 21-7 with just under five minutes left in the second quarter. Three plays after Devin Smith caught a 47-yard pass to the Oregon five on third-and-12, Jones scored on a sneak.

Oregon would make it a game, but the Buckeyes did what they did all year — answer the challenge.

"We've been faced with adversity all year long, on the field and off the field," tight end

The Oregon defense had trouble corralling Cardale Jones, the 250-pound quarterback who was making just his third start. (Jonathan Quilter/Dispatch)

Jeff Heuerman said. "Those turnovers were just another example of adversity we had to overcome. It's truly special. It's the best feeling I've ever had."

It's one that Jones, in particular, couldn't have imagined when he was buried on the depth chart behind Miller and J.T. Barrett.

"Going back to camp in August, everybody counted us out when our Heisman Trophy quarterback went down," Jones said. "Then when the first College Football Playoff rankings came out, we were No. 16. Long story short, we weren't supposed to be here.

"All the odds were stacked against us through the whole season, and for us to be sitting here as national champs, it not only means a lot to me, but our community, Buckeye Nation and our hometowns."

As the confetti fell around him, center Jacoby Boren soaked it in.

"I'm speechless," he said. "We're national champions. It's a once-in-a-lifetime opportunity."

Given how young this team is, don't be so sure. ∎

Above: Defensive lineman Adolphus Washington sacks Oregon quarterback Marcus Mariota. Opposite: Ezekiel Elliott jumps over Oregon defensive backs Tyree Robinson, right, and Chris Seisay for a chunk of his 246 rushing yards. (Jonathan Quilter/Dispatch)

"WE KNEW THAT OUR O-LINE WAS BIGGER AND MORE PHYSICAL THAN THEIR D-LINE, AND WE JUST HAD TO PUNCH THEM IN THE MOUTH." — EZEKIEL ELLIOTT

Ezekiel Elliott leaves Oregon defenders in the dust as he ties the game in the first quarter. (Eamon Queeney/Dispatch)

ELLIOTT RUSHES TO OFFENSIVE MVP HONORS

Running Back Carries for 246 Yards to Pace Buckeyes

By Tim May

Ezekiel Elliott took a few tentative steps at the start of the College Football Playoff championship game.

But once the Ohio State running back got it going, he did so in a big way, with his 246 yards and four touchdowns rushing leading the way in Ohio State's 42-20 win over Oregon.

Elliott was named offensive most valuable player for his effort, which included a career-high 36 carries and touchdown runs of 33, 9, 2 and 1 yards.

OSU safety Tyvis Powell was named defensive MVP after a performance in which he had nine tackles and broke up a pass.

Besides lifting Ohio State to its sixth national title, Elliott launched himself into second place on the list of best rushing seasons at OSU.

He finished his sophomore season with 1,878 yards, just shy of Eddie George's record of 1,927 yards, set in 1995. Elliott entered the game in fourth place on the single-season list but passed Archie Griffin (1,695 in 1974) and Keith Byars (1,764 in 1984) along the way.

Elliott racked up his total in 15 games, while George played 13 games in 1995, and Griffin and Byars played in 12 games in '74 and '84, respectively.

Despite the extra games, Elliott's strong finish to the 2014 season was as impressive as any running back's in school history as the St. Louis native gained 924 yards in the Buckeyes' final five games.

"You got to credit 'the slobs,' because they're the ones that pave the way," Elliott said, referring to the nickname for the offensive linemen led by guards Pat Elflein and Billy Price.

Elliott and the offense were slow out of the gate, but his 33-yard touchdown run at 4:36 of the first quarter woke up the Buckeyes, and the OSU-dominant crowd of 85,689 at AT&T Stadium got into it in a loud way.

George, his record safe for at least another year, said

it was obvious that Elliott and the Buckeyes were coming on down the stretch.

"The way this offensive line has meshed and jelled is fantastic," George said.

George laughed when asked how many yards he might have gained in his Heisman Trophy-winning season of 1995 if he had been able to play 15 games rather than 13.

"I sat out the second or a lot of the second half in quite a few of those games," George said. "I definitely would have gotten over 2,000."

With the Buckeyes and Ducks playing 15 games in the longest season in major-college football history, George said it was a lot to ask for a college team and running back. As he met with players during the days before the game, he came away with a general feeling that some players were being worn down a bit — "running on fumes," as he put it.

But Elliott had plenty of gas for the Buckeyes' biggest games of the year. He rushed for 220 yards against Wisconsin in the Big Ten championship game, 230 against Alabama in the national playoff semifinal in the Sugar Bowl and 246 against Oregon.

"Everybody does their job, and nothing would be possible without that team effort," Elliott said. "The O-line, they came out, they played their butts off and they paved the way for me. … I feel blessed."

The performance drew raves from Elliott's teammates and coaches.

"Wow. Wow," Ohio State running backs coach Stan Drayton said. "The passion you see with this kid running the football, it's all about his teammates, it's not about him … and I love him to death for that. He is a selfless kid."

OSU coach Urban Meyer, meanwhile, referred to Elliott as "the most underrated back in America."

"He's one of the best post-contact yard guys I've ever been around, and on top of that he's a great human being." ■

Having surpassed 200 rushing yards for the third straight game, Ezekiel Elliott was the obvious MVP choice. (Adam Cairns/Dispatch)

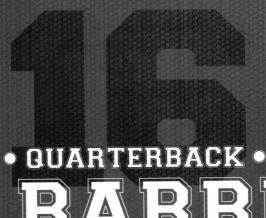

• QUARTERBACK •
J.T. BARRETT

Barrett's Life Story Revolves Around Dogged Determination
By Bill Rabinowitz • August 30, 2014

A person's life can be measured in numbers, but it is revealed in stories.

And oh, the stories that those who know him best like to tell about J.T. Barrett, Ohio State's new starting quarterback.

Let's start with one from the first year Barrett played football.

Joe Barrett can tell you about that. His son — formally named Joe Thomas Barrett IV — announced his football ambition almost from the start. J.T., the middle of Joe and Stacy Barrett's three sons, was about 6.

He was wearing his football helmet and holding a ball in the Barretts' home in Wichita Falls, Texas, when he made a declaration.

"He said, 'This is what I want to do,'" Joe recalled. "He said we're not going to have to pay for his education because this here is what he wants to do. We just laughed at him. We looked at him like he was a little crazy. I said, 'OK, son.'"

The Barretts' skepticism was understandable. Football wasn't really in J.T.'s genes. Joe played basketball and ran track as a kid in Buna, Texas.

"I've never played a lick of football in my life," he said.

Stacy, now a nurse, also was an athlete. Joe said J.T. gets his competitiveness from her.

"Me, I'm competitive, but not to that extreme," he said.

J.T. excelled at football right away. He was a two-way star, with running back his main position on offense. But in fifth grade, after a summer of eating too much, J.T. was 15 pounds above the weight limit for his youth football league. He could play defense, but unless he dropped the weight, he wouldn't be able to carry the ball on offense.

Joe, an electronics technician who has served 28 years in the Army Reserve, is an early riser by nature. So J.T. had a solution.

He begged his father to wake him at 5 a.m. and take him to the gym to work off the weight.

"I was like, 'Oh, my Lord,' but he would get up so he would get that weight off," Stacy Barrett said. "That's his determination. He lost the weight."

Joe remembers seeing adults at the gym, particularly older ones, giving him a look when they saw J.T. there so early. Overbearing father, they thought, based on their gazes.

That's when J.T. decided to silence them.

"He told them, 'I woke my daddy up. I want to work out,'" Joe said. "If he's willing to be dedicated like that and work to achieve a goal, what's my job? To support him."

At about that age, John Hatch moved to Wichita Falls. He and J.T. became best friends from the first time they

Before suffering a season-ending injury, J.T. Barrett threw for 34 touchdowns during the 2014 season. (Fred Squillante/Dispatch)

played football at recess. J.T. became the quarterback, and Hatch was his receiver.

"We've always been on the same page and always loved playing football," Hatch said.

From the time he started playing with Barrett, Hatch said, their teams didn't lose a game until their sophomore year of high school. That season, Barrett led Rider High to the state playoffs. He didn't have the strongest arm and wasn't the swiftest runner. But his intangibles — leadership, maturity, selflessness — were obvious to everybody.

"The team just turned to him," Hatch said. "At team meetings on Thursday night when we talked about what to prepare for, he always had the right thing to say.

"When things were crumbling, everyone would turn to J.T. for what to do. He helped you really understand that it's really more about team than themselves. That's just a God-given thing that he's always had. His mind was on a whole different level than the rest of us."

"He does have," Stacy Barrett said, "a little bit of an old soul."

Entering Barrett's senior year, the expectation at Rider was that the Raiders would bring home a state championship.

"In Wichita Falls, everything is built up to the high school team," Hatch said. "Everyone goes to the high school games, and it's just like going to the pro games. Everyone loves it."

But midway through his season, Barrett suffered a tear of the anterior cruciate ligament in his left knee.

"It was rough on him at first, but then he handled it well," Hatch said. "He was at every practice. He was still the leader of the team even though he couldn't play. He kept the younger quarterbacks' heads on straight.

"He handled it well. That's J.T. I'm not sure how he does it."

Those qualities are what drew Ohio State to him. He was the first quarterback that the Buckeyes signed under coach Urban Meyer, with offensive coordinator Tom Herman doing the heavy lifting in recruiting.

Barrett was a four-star prospect, but he probably would have stayed in or near Texas until he received a fateful call.

"He wanted to stay close to home, but when *the* Urban Meyer called him, that was about a done deal," Stacy Barrett said. "He called me, and he was like, 'Mom (in a low voice), guess who called me. '*The* Urban Meyer.'"

The plan was for Barrett to spend this season as Braxton Miller's backup after taking 2013 to rehab his knee, and then compete for a starting job next season. Miller's shoulder injury changed that timetable.

Is he ready? If it's a matter of determination, well, let Hatch provide one more story. It was just before their senior year started, they decided to hold a Madden football video-game tournament at Hatch's house. The prize would be a small gold trophy that Hatch's dad had won as a kid.

Barrett and Hatch won their games to set up their finals match in the morning. That night, they played a practice game, which Hatch won easily.

"He stayed up all night practicing," Hatch said.

The next morning, Barrett won.

"He beat me like I stole something," Hatch said.

Barrett got the trophy, but he decided to give it to Hatch. It wasn't a magnanimous gesture.

"He said he wanted me to keep it by my bed so that when I wake up in the morning," Hatch said with a laugh, "I can look at it and remember that he beat me." ■

J.T. Barrett hurdles Indiana cornerback Rashard Fant for a chunk of his 78 rushing yards during the 42-27 victory. (Eric Albrecht/Dispatch)

OHIO STATE 34, NAVY 17
August 30, 2014 • Baltimore, Maryland

RIGHTING THE SHIP

Ohio State's Two Fourth-Quarter TDs Help Overcome Sluggish Start

By Bill Rabinowitz

With Ohio State clinging to an uncomfortable three-point lead early in the fourth quarter, the offense faced fourth-and-1 at the Navy 45-yard line.

Ezekiel Elliott had been stuffed in the same situation a quarter earlier. This time, he dived for a first down — barely.

Three plays later, Elliott scored on a 10-yard run to allow Ohio State to exhale comfortably for the first time in a 34-17 season-opening victory in front of a mostly pro-Buckeyes crowd of 57,579 at M&T Bank Stadium.

But that fourth-down play summed up the afternoon. Even when things worked out, the Buckeyes flirted with disaster.

A Navy defensive end crashed in from his spot. Had the quarterback, redshirt freshman J.T. Barrett, responded correctly, he would have bounced outside and run for an easy first down. Instead, it was close enough for Navy to challenge, though unsuccessfully.

"He didn't read it correctly," Ohio State offensive coordinator Tom Herman said. "When the call is to read the end and the end is screaming down there, you've got to go with what the play is designed to do."

Herman was quick to add that Barrett did much more right than wrong in his debut replacing injured starter Braxton Miller. Except for a brain-cramp interception near the Navy goal line in the first half, Barrett lived up to his billing as an efficient, poised

leader. He finished 12 of 15 for 226 yards and two touchdowns.

"We're going to enjoy this win," Barrett said, "but definitely there's a little relief as far as myself getting the first one out of the way and getting a win under my belt."

Barrett's 50 yards rushing also made him Ohio State's leading rusher, which isn't such a good thing. The Buckeyes' offensive line, which had four new starters, struggled to open holes and protect Barrett when he passed, particularly in the first half.

The Buckeyes had the ball inside the Midshipmen's 12-yard line three times in the first half and got only three points out of them, to trail 7–6 at halftime. Ohio State almost always cashed in from the red zone the past two years, when it could rely on Miller, Carlos Hyde and the old offensive line.

"It was very concerning early," Herman said. "I was reaching into the call sheet trying to figure out any throws or runs we could do to mask the deficiencies we had. We challenged them at halftime."

Meanwhile, Ohio State's defense struggled against Navy's triple-option offense, executed with precision by quarterback Keenan Reynolds. The Midshipmen ran for 370 yards, the most the Buckeyes have surrendered since a 1995 loss to Michigan.

"We came into the game knowing that Navy's not a pushover team," said defensive tackle Michael Bennett. "They're a good team, and they run the triple

J.T. Barrett, who threw for 226 yards and two touchdowns, looks to pass during the first start of his Ohio State career. (Barbara J. Perenic/Dispatch)

option to perfection. It was frustrating to see the pitch player getting free a lot, but they were doing a good job (cut-blocking), and we were having a hard time sticking with them. You have to give props to Navy."

Two huge plays kept the Buckeyes afloat in the third quarter. Redshirt linebacker Darron Lee scooped up a fumble — caused when Joey Bosa hit Reynolds as he made a pitch — and ran 61 yards for a touchdown.

Then, after Navy retook the lead on a four-play, 84-yard drive, Barrett hit Devin Smith for an 80-yard score to put Ohio State back ahead 20-14. A Navy field goal cut Ohio State's lead to three before Elliott converted the fourth-down dive to keep alive the drive that made it a two-possession lead.

The Buckeyes then got a three-and-out for just the third time. They added their final touchdown with 2:09 left on a 70-yard drive against a worn-down Navy defense.

"I was proud of our guys for three quarters," Navy coach Ken Niumatalolo said. "We were fighting our guts out. We didn't finish."

Ohio State did, overcoming the deficiencies it showed until then.

"We found out a lot of things about some of our kids — things we probably didn't handle the best the last couple years," defensive coordinator Luke Fickell said. "We came to the sidelines in adverse situations, and we saw a lot of grown-up guys today. Guys had great demeanors and believed in what we were doing. We took a step today."

The Buckeyes have their home opener next week against Virginia Tech.

"Obviously, with the team we have next, we have a lot of work to do," coach Urban Meyer said. "But we'll take this win. I'm very proud of our guys for fighting through the second half and doing what they did. The best thing about this game was we won, and it's in the rearview mirror." ∎

Running back Ezekiel Elliott finds the hole for a chunk of his 44 rushing yards during the season-opening victory. (Kyle Robertson/Dispatch)

VIRGINIA TECH 35, OHIO STATE 21
September 6, 2014 • Columbus, Ohio

LATE-NIGHT FRIGHT

OSU Offense Folds Under Pressure

By Bill Rabinowitz

The largest crowd in Ohio Stadium history witnessed a clunker.

Hoping to redeem the Big Ten's reputation on a miserable day for the conference, Ohio State couldn't deliver.

The Buckeyes rallied from a 14-point halftime deficit to tie the score, but Virginia Tech landed the knockout blows to beat No. 8 Ohio State 35–21 and hand Urban Meyer the first regular-season loss of his Buckeyes tenure.

After decisive losses by Michigan State and Michigan in marquee games yesterday and a near-upset of Nebraska by McNeese State, Ohio State was the conference's last hope for an impressive victory.

When the Buckeyes scored two touchdowns to erase a 21-7 halftime deficit, they seemed poised to do it.

But Bucky Hodges caught a 10-yard touchdown pass from Michael Brewer with 8:44 left, and the Buckeyes' offense couldn't answer. A 63-yard interception return by Donovan Riley with 46 seconds left clinched it.

Thanks to stadium expansion in the South Stands, a record crowd at Ohio Stadium of 107,517 watched the prime-time game. They had reason to enter the Horseshoe confident. Ohio State hadn't lost a home game to an unranked nonconference opponent since losing to Stanford and Florida State in consecutive weeks in 1982.

Virginia Tech (2-0) had never beaten a team ranked eighth or higher on the road. After losing a total of 11 games the past two years, the Hokies were optimistic that they were ready to return to national prominence.

They provided concrete evidence, though they got plenty of help from the mistake-prone hosts.

In his home debut as starting quarterback, J.T. Barrett completed only 9 of 29 passes for 219 yards with three interceptions. But it would be unfair to pin the loss on him. He seldom had time to throw, thanks to pressure designed by Virginia Tech defensive coordinator Bud Foster that overwhelmed the Buckeyes' rebuilt offensive line with seven sacks.

Barrett's receivers had key drops and had trouble gaining separation. Because of that, Virginia Tech could stay with its man-to-man pass defense and clog up the line of scrimmage to disrupt the run game. Ohio State's running backs gained only 58 yards in 13 carries. "I don't think our wide receivers played well," Meyer said. "That's a good secondary. They put their corners on islands, and we didn't expose it."

Still, Ohio State (1-1) had a chance. Down by 14, the Buckeyes closed to a touchdown on a 53-yard touchdown catch by Michael Thomas late in the third quarter.

The Buckeyes tied the score with 11:40 left in the fourth quarter, set up by their defense. Defensive end

Running back Dontre Wilson makes an acrobatic one-handed catch against Virginia Tech cornerback Chuck Clark for a 40-yard gain during the second quarter. (Kyle Robertson/Dispatch)

Joey Bosa drilled Hokies quarterback Michael Brewer, jarring the ball free. Rashad Frazier recovered at the Virginia Tech 15.

Ezekiel Elliott scored from that distance two plays later.

After Hodges' touchdown, the Buckeyes had three possessions to tie. The first went nowhere. The second ended on a third-and-18 interception with less than five minutes left.

The Buckeyes got their final chance after A.J. Hughes missed a 46-yard field goal with 3:06 left. Barrett scrambled for a first down on third-and-20, and the Buckeyes got to the Virginia Tech 45.

But after the Hokies' final sack, Barrett's pass intended for Corey Smith was intercepted by Riley and returned for a score.

Ohio State didn't look like it would have much of a chance based on the first half, when Barrett's play was about the only thing that went right.

The redshirt freshman quarterback ran for all of Ohio State's nonpenalty yardage on its only scoring drive. He also hit Devin Smith and Dontre Wilson on long completions.

"Gutsy performance," Meyer said of Barrett.

But he got little help.

The other two phases of the game were even shoddier. Ohio State spent all offseason installing a pass defense designed to challenge every pass.

Brewer had little trouble dissecting it. The Hokies converted their first five third-down situations in their first two touchdown drives.

The Buckeyes' kicking game was worse. Freshman Sean Nuernberger missed two field goals, including a 27-yarder. Cameron Johnston shanked a punt that set up one of the Virginia Tech touchdown drives. The Buckeyes had a block-in-the-back penalty and a late-hit call on kicks and allowed a 35-yard punt return. ■

Virginia Tech defensive tackle Corey Marshall takes down quarterback J.T. Barrett for a third-quarter sack. (Kyle Robertson/Dispatch)

OHIO STATE 66, KENT STATE 0
September 13, 2014 • Columbus, Ohio

OVER IN A FLASH

Buckeyes Find Cure for Their Ills

By Bill Rabinowitz

It was a check-mark game for Ohio State, this 66-0 victory over Kent State.

Shake off disappointment from the Virginia Tech game with a quick start? Check.

Have the defense show that it could get off the field on third down? Check.

Get the Buckeyes' playmakers a chance to strut their stuff after two weeks of being mostly stifled? Check.

What does it all mean? Check back in several more weeks.

Yesterday's victory before a near-capacity crowd of 104,404 at Ohio Stadium lacked any semblance of drama. The Buckeyes led 24-0 after less than 16 minutes and 45-0 at halftime before emptying the bench for most of the second half.

Redshirt freshman quarterback J.T. Barrett threw for 312 yards — most by a Buckeye since Terrelle Pryor's 334 against Indiana in 2010 — and tied Kenny Guiton's school record with six touchdown passes.

Ohio State outgained Kent State 628-126.

Yes, this was ugly. But to the No. 22 Buckeyes (2-1), it was needed comfort food after a 35-21 loss to Virginia Tech last week.

"After last week, we felt heartbroken," running back Ezekiel Elliott said. "We had a sick feeling in our stomach. We had to come out today for ourselves

and Buckeye Nation. Today was what we needed. We needed to get some momentum on offense, and we got that today. I think we're on a good track."

Certainly, Kent State (0-3) was an ideal opponent for that. The Golden Flashes tried to use a variation of the "Bear" defense, clogging the middle, that Virginia Tech used.

Kent State is not Virginia Tech. Ohio State got chunks of yardage at a time on the ground, and Barrett lived up to his distributor tag by completing passes to eight different receivers in the first quarter.

"Virginia Tech was making us throw the ball downfield, (and showing) things we hadn't seen," Barrett said, "and we didn't do a great job of adjusting to that as the game went along. Today, we came in with a pretty good idea of what they were going to do and played to our game plan all week, and it worked out for us."

The Buckeyes scored on every drive in the first half except for an interception that deflected off of Michael Thomas near the Kent State goal line on Ohio State's third possession. But Thomas redeemed himself with two touchdown catches, including a 63-yarder to make it 31-0.

The Buckeyes didn't punt until less than six minutes remained in the game.

Quarterback J.T. Barrett, who tied a school record with six touchdown passes during a game, prepares to throw during the third quarter. (Kyle Robertson/Dispatch)

"Early in the first half, I wanted to throw a lot," coach Urban Meyer said. "I wanted to force (Barrett) and receivers to make plays."

The defense was just as dominant. Ohio State got interceptions from Joshua Perry, Tyvis Powell and freshman Erick Smith. Kent State never got beyond the Ohio State 41-yard line. On third down, a problem for the Ohio State defense against Virginia Tech, the Flashes converted 2 of 14 chances.

Barrett played only one series in the second half, throwing a 3-yard touchdown pass to Jalin Marshall on his final throw.

Cardale Jones replaced him, surrounded by backups the rest of the way.

"Obviously, (we had) a little talent advantage," Meyer said, "but we had to have a game like this. Normally, that's a first game, especially when you have a young quarterback and a young offensive line. But I'm glad we played like we did."

Next, after a bye week, is Cincinnati, which will be a much sterner test. The Bearcats rolled past Toledo on Friday 58-34.

Kent State coach Paul Haynes is a former Ohio State assistant. He understands how Buckeyes fans react to a loss, and he also knew what he was up against.

"Those are (the weight of) expectations here — you lose one game and the world falls apart," he said. "They are still a top-10 football team. At the end of November, they probably will be fighting for a championship." ∎

Wide receiver Michael Thomas scores a 14-yard touchdown for the first points in Ohio State's blowout victory. (Jenna Watson/Dispatch)

• HEAD COACH •
URBAN MEYER

Meyer Helps Team Overcome Losses of Braxton Miller and Noah Spence
By Tim May • September 20, 2014

A college coach learns early to roll with the punches, but they still hurt. Some pack a wallop. Just ask Urban Meyer.

"But name a team that's never had an issue," Meyer said. "That team doesn't exist."

In early August, his third Ohio State team was ranked No. 5 in the Associated Press preseason poll. Despite the plethora of new starters on offense and defense, the Buckeyes sported the return of Braxton Miller, one of the country's premier playmakers at quarterback.

All-Big Ten defensive end Noah Spence was due back in Game 3 after serving the final two games of a drug-related suspension that began with last season's Orange Bowl.

A pre-Big Ten schedule that included a game with Virginia Tech appeared to be quite manageable. So did the dive into conference play headed toward a game at Michigan State on Nov. 8.

Then came the uppercut: Miller, rebounding from shoulder surgery after the Orange Bowl loss to Clemson, suffered a dislocated shoulder while throwing a pass in his first significant practice of the preseason.

And the left cross: It was learned last week that Spence tested positive for the drug Ecstasy a second time. The junior, the Buckeyes' leading sacker a year ago with 8.0, was suspended immediately and, pending appeal, might have played his last college game.

After his first failed test, Spence said his drink had been spiked at a party. The second time, he came clean to his parents and Meyer about his addiction and he now is seeking treatment and counseling.

Past the obvious hit the team took in terms of losing two elite players, Miller and Spence are two of Meyer's favorites. It's a natural reaction to feel for them, despite their opposite plights.

"Noah, if you took 100 guys on the team, he would have been near the bottom of the list of any guy I thought would have had an issue like that," Meyer said. "He's a good student. He comes from a good family.

"We're usually knee-deep into all of these kids, but I never — that was all news to me when that broke.

"That was a sucker punch, boy, when I got that phone call."

But he rolled with it. He had to.

The anguish he felt when Miller was injured was visceral, and more than just for what the quarterback's talent obviously meant to the team. Meyer also knew of the work that Miller had put in over the years in general, and the previous six months in particular, to prepare for his senior season.

"So you just see a guy who is like a member of your family go down, and you're like, 'Ugggh,'" Meyer said at the time. "Your gut starts to hurt. You go over to see if he's OK. It was a tough situation."

But the coach must roll with the punches because all eyes — those of the players, assistant coaches and fans — are on him to show the way, regardless.

Urban Meyer raises the Stagg Championship Trophy after winning his first Big Ten championship. (Kyle Robertson/Dispatch)

Life was a lot simpler in the days before Meyer became a head coach, because "as a young assistant coach coming up, you've just got your little group of players to deal with," he said.

But stepping to the top rung meant the posse suddenly grew into a cavalry, with all looking to him for guidance through challenges and tough times. He had big plans about what he wanted to do on offense and defense, but quickly found out there was so much more to it than X's and O's.

"As a new head coach at 36 years old at Bowling Green, my first year, it was like 'You've got to be kidding.' Every day it seemed there was something you had to deal with," Meyer said. "Like with study table, there was some kind of issue. Or there was an issue with a player's family. It just seemed there was an off-the-field issue constantly that could take away from your focus, and it did."

Advice from coaching mentors such as Earle Bruce, Lou Holtz and others helped him sort through it all, but only years on the job and mileage could add the compartmentalizing factor a head coach must have.

The physical and psychological strain of being the head coach got to him at Florida the year after he had guided the Gators to their second national championship in three seasons. He resigned abruptly two days after Christmas in 2009, only to decide to return, then resign again after the 2010 season.

That journey has been chronicled many times, because he just as abruptly opted to return to coaching and Ohio State in late 2011, after less than one year out of the grind. Though he made the famous "pink contract" with his wife, Shelley, and three children to lead a more-balanced life, especially in terms of dealing with the stress, he missed more than anything else the relationships with the players, something for which he feels better equipped than ever before.

"It's just part of the maturing cycle for a head coach," Meyer said. "You're dealing with 125 players from all kinds of different backgrounds. It's part of the challenge, and things aren't always going to go right."

While OSU fans rued the fall to Virginia Tech as new quarterback J.T. Barrett, a young offensive line and an overhauled defense got their baptism under fire, Meyer had to deal with the now and the future, telling the media that he thinks this can still be a championship team but that there is obvious work to do.

Losses always have hit him like a Mike Tyson hook, and he makes no apology for that, but the show must go on.

"At Bowling Green, I actually put a sign up over the staff room door: 'Don't tell me the problem. Tell me the solution,'" Meyer said. "Problems are always going to arise, whether it's injury, or a player not being available, or a challenge in recruiting. The question is, 'What's the solution?' That's where the time should be spent."

Meyer didn't erupt, at least to the players, in the days after the loss to Virginia Tech, left tackle Taylor Decker said. But he did speak in stern terms about the challenge they all faced.

"It's not like he's going to be in there exploding, screaming at guys," Decker said. "I mean, everybody has got to be accountable for their own job. His approach when something like that happens is 'We weren't good enough in some aspects.' So we've got to improve and it gives you the chance to reflect."

Decker further said of Meyer's demeanor, "He is definitely an intense guy, but he's also very grounded at the same time, and he's realistic. I've never experienced him really exploding in a situation where it didn't seem fitting. … He knows what he's doing." ■

Urban Meyer directs his team before defeating Penn State in double overtime. (Brooke LaValley/Dispatch)

OHIO STATE 50, CINCINNATI 28
September 27, 2014 • Columbus, Ohio

LIGHTS OUT

OSU Dominates Up Front, Totals 710 Yards Against In-State Foe

By Bill Rabinowitz

No one expected Cincinnati to be a typical in-state patsy for Ohio State.

With a high-powered offense led by quarterback Gunner Kiel, the Bearcats figured to have a puncher's chance against the Buckeyes.

A few Cincinnati haymakers did stagger Ohio State, but the Buckeyes' offense overwhelmed the Bearcats in a 50-28 victory in front of a record Ohio Stadium crowd of 108,362.

The No. 22 Buckeyes (3-1) had a school-record 45 first downs and briefly broke the school record for total yards before a late 20-yard loss caused them to settle for 710 yards, eight short of the record.

Redshirt freshman quarterback J.T. Barrett again played with calmness and toughness, passing for 330 yards and four touchdowns.

Ezekiel Elliott ran 28 times for a career-high 182 yards and a touchdown.

Barrett was seldom touched in the pocket, and Buckeye runners were often untouched for several yards.

"We're an offensive-line-driven team, and they won the game for us," coach Urban Meyer said. "They controlled the line."

And, yet, because Kiel passed for 352 yards and four touchdowns — three on long scores to Chris Moore — Cincinnati (2-1) made it a game.

Ohio State led 30-7 early in the second quarter before the Bearcats closed to 33-28 on a 78-yard touchdown catch by Moore in the third quarter.

Meyer summed up his mood at that moment in one word.

"Pissed," he said. "Great teams don't do that. I don't want to take anything away from UC because UC is legitimate, probably the best throwing team we've faced since we've been here."

But this was not what Meyer had in mind when he hired Chris Ash to fix Ohio State's porous pass defense. The Buckeyes spent all offseason preparing for a test like this.

"Defensively, we're back to the drawing board in pass coverage," Meyer said. "A couple of corners got beat, and we gave up big plays. We've got to get that fixed. You can't play championship football until it gets fixed."

It could have been worse.

After a field goal by Ohio State pushed its lead to 36-28, Cincinnati got the ball back. From the Bearcats' 40, Kiel threw deep to Johnny Holton. Buckeyes cornerback Eli Apple grabbed Holton before Holton returned the favor, and a flag was thrown — on UC for offensive pass interference.

Cincinnati coach Tommy Tuberville was livid, and the call proved to be the final turning point in a game that had many. The 15-yard penalty put the

While garnering part of Ohio State's 380 rushing yards, quarterback J.T. Barrett avoids Cincinnati defensive lineman Brandon Mitchell. (Adam Cairns/Dispatch)

Bearcats in a hole they couldn't escape, and they were forced to punt.

Ohio State then did what it did for most of the game. It moved the ball almost at will. Barrett threw to a wide-open Dontre Wilson for a 24-yard touchdown, and the Buckeyes were never threatened again.

The good and bad for Ohio State surfaced early. On the game's fourth play, Moore beat safety Vonn Bell in man-to-man coverage for a 60-yard touchdown.

But Ohio State's offense played almost flawlessly for the next 16 minutes, scoring touchdowns on its first four drives. Ohio State had 18 first downs on its first 32 snaps.

The defense added a safety when Joey Bosa drilled Kiel, forcing a fumble that the Bearcats swatted out of the end zone.

When Evan Spencer scored on a 19-yard pass with 12:34 left in the second quarter for a 30-7 lead, it looked like the blowout was on.

But then the Buckeyes got sloppy. Freshman running back Curtis Samuel fumbled at the Bearcats' 42, and Cincinnati capitalized. Kiel threw to Holton for a 19-yard touchdown with 5:23 left in the half.

Ohio State drove to Cincinnati's 45 before three straight Barrett passes were dropped, the last one an easy toss to Smith for what would have been a first down.

Cameron Johnston's punt was downed at Cincinnati's 3 with 1:51 left, and when the Bearcats took their time on their first three snaps, it looked like they were content to run out the clock. Ohio State sure seemed to think so.

But after a first down, Kiel threw deep to Moore, who beat Apple in one-on-one coverage and outran him to the end zone with 26 seconds left for an 83-yard touchdown.

The game was on, but Ohio State had the answers when it needed them. ∎

Wide receiver Devin Smith hauls in a 34-yard touchdown, the final score for either team during Ohio State's emphatic 50-28 victory. (Adam Cairns/Dispatch)

OHIO STATE 52, MARYLAND 24
October 4, 2014 • College Park, Maryland

WALK IN THE PARK

Fast Start Keys Buckeyes' Victory Against Terps

By Bill Rabinowitz

Urban Meyer was not going to take any chances. Bedtime was 9 p.m. on Friday for Ohio State's players.

Meyer knew that sold-out Byrd Stadium would be hopping yesterday for Maryland's first home game as a member of the Big Ten. The Buckeyes coach spent much of last week doing everything he could to ensure that his players would be ready, including getting enough sleep for their conference opener.

He needn't have worried. Ohio State jumped on Maryland with two early touchdowns, and its much-maligned pass defense had four interceptions in the 20th-ranked Buckeyes' 52-24 victory.

"When you go on the road for a noon game, sometimes it's the middle of the first quarter before they wake up," Meyer said. "The other team jumps on you, and all of a sudden it's 7-0, and you're playing uphill the entire game. We went nuts this week with that. Our coaching staff, I was grinding them pretty hard on Tuesday, Wednesday and Thursday about a quick start."

Meyer felt reassured yesterday morning when he saw the body language of his players. If there was any doubt, it was erased when the Maryland student section did an "Overrated!" chant during pregame.

"He came in yelling about that," defensive end Joey Bosa said about Meyer, adding with a laugh, "I can't really say what he said."

The Buckeyes (4-1, 1-0), or at least tight end Jeff Heuerman in comments that got considerable attention, said they wanted to introduce the Terrapins to Big Ten football. Maryland (4-2, 1-1) had soundly defeated Indiana 37-15 in its Big Ten debut, but the Terps learned that Ohio State is not Indiana.

Redshirt freshman quarterback J.T. Barrett continued his impressive play by completing 18 of 23 passes for 264 yards and four touchdowns. Ezekiel Elliott ran for 139 yards.

The Buckeyes finished with a balanced offense — 269 rushing yards and 264 passing — but they imposed their will early with their ground game. They took the opening kickoff and drove 75 yards in eight plays, all but one of them runs, to take a 7-0 lead, and moved just as efficiently on their next possession for another touchdown.

"We wanted to set the tone and let them know we were going to run the ball on them," offensive tackle Taylor Decker said. "We try to be an offensive line-driven team, and the way the backs have been running, we want to establish that."

Led by Bosa, the defensive line was even more dominating. Ohio State sacked Maryland quarterback C.J. Brown three times in the first half before Terps coach Randy Edsall replaced him with Caleb Rowe.

Maryland's running game was mostly a nonfactor, and the Buckeyes harassed both quarterbacks when

Wide receiver Michael Thomas (with ball) celebrates his 25-yard touchdown in the second quarter with running back Jalin Marshall. (Chris Russell/Dispatch)

they took deep drops and sniffed out the Terrapins' screen-passing game.

Except for a 60-yard completion on a missed assignment, Maryland's longest play from scrimmage was a 25-yarder. And that from an offense that had been averaging almost 37 points a game.

The Buckeyes extended their lead to 21-3 on a spectacular catch by Michael Thomas in the back left corner of the end zone. Cornerback William Likely had tight coverage, but Thomas reached above him to make the grab while tiptoeing to stay in bounds.

"I knew I had a 5-7 corner, and I trust Michael Thomas to go get the ball because he's 6-3," Barrett said.

Only once after that did Maryland threaten to make it a game. The Terps drove 75 yards for a touchdown late in the second quarter to cut Ohio State's lead to 24-10, and then forced a three-and-out.

But Cameron Johnston's 69-yard punt was downed at Maryland's 7-yard line. On the next play, linebacker Darron Lee intercepted Brown's short pass. Lee fumbled, but freshman linebacker Raekwon McMillan scooped it up and ran it to the 1.

Barrett then threw to tight end Nick Vannett for a touchdown to give the Buckeyes a 21-point halftime lead.

The teams traded two touchdowns apiece in the second half until McMillan intercepted a tipped pass and ran 19 yards for the game's final score with just under nine minutes left.

"I'm very pleased with our performance," said Meyer, whose team is off this week, its second bye in four weeks. "I know it wasn't perfect and that's what you strive to be, but (it was impressive) against a team that's 4-1 and we have a lot of respect for."

Edsall had billed the game as an opportunity to show how ready the Terrapins were to make an impact in their new conference.

"What we found out," he said, "is that Ohio State is a very good football team. That's the standard we're going to have to reach here at Maryland."

They weren't close on this day. ■

Wide receiver Devin Smith snares a 30-yard touchdown catch to give Ohio State a 38-10 lead in the third quarter. (Brooke LaValley/Dispatch)

63

• DEFENSIVE LINEMAN •

MICHAEL BENNETT

Move From Nose Guard to Defensive Tackle Benefits Senior Leader

By Bill Rabinowitz • December 20, 2014

Michael Bennett was having a perfectly nice, solid senior season for the Ohio State Buckeyes. Then something happened. Really, it was more than one thing. But in the Buckeyes' stretch drive toward a spot in the College Football Playoff, Bennett became much more than a nice, solid player. He became a beast.

Through Ohio State's first eight games, the defensive tackle had three tackles for a loss. In the Buckeyes' last five games, he had nine tackles behind the line of scrimmage, including four in the 59-0 rout of Wisconsin in the Big Ten championship game.

"About six weeks ago, Michael Bennett flipped a switch," co-defensive coordinator Chris Ash said. "Something changed. He's become a much better leader. He's become a much better practice player. He's become a much better game player. Everybody else has fed off of that."

Bennett credits a change in his position and also his mindset for the improvement that helped him earn third-team Associated Press All-America honors. And against Wisconsin, another factor drove him.

Now the Buckeyes are preparing for their toughest task of the year. They will play Alabama in the Sugar Bowl on New Year's Day. The Crimson Tide is a nine-point favorite, but the Buckeyes are undaunted.

"I'm excited because as long as I've been in college, people have seen Alabama as that unbeatable entity, the top notch of college football," Bennett said. "I think we can compete with them and give them a heckuva game, and I think we can win. I'm really excited to prove to the country that Ohio State is the real deal."

• • • • • • •

Bennett's parents, Connie and Mike, are West Point graduates. They instilled discipline and a work ethic in Michael and his two younger sisters. Early on, it was apparent to his parents that Michael wasn't an average kid.

Defensive tackle Michael Bennett pressures Penn Sate quarterback Christian Hackenberg during Ohio State's double-overtime victory. (Chris Russell/Dispatch)

"It goes way back to early Montessori, kindergarten, first grade," Mike Bennett said. "We saw things in him that made us know he was pretty sharp. Even now, I think he could be a movie critic if he wanted to be just because of how he analyzes things."

Everything came easily to him — in sports, in school and socially — and that might not always have been a blessing. It wasn't until Urban Meyer took over as coach after Bennett's freshman season that he realized — or was made to realize — that good wasn't good enough.

"Everybody has to grow up eventually, and I was fortunate to have the coaching staff I did," Bennett said. "They forced me to grow up and forced me to take the role of wanting to be great and not needing someone to push me to do what it takes to be great. Now I feel I have that drive and that desire."

Bennett blossomed as a junior last year before stingers that affected his arm and neck caused him to tail off late in the season.

Then this year, Bennett got off to an unspectacular start. Ohio State had two interior linemen spots. Bennett was asked to play nose guard, close to the ball, instead of the 3-technique tackle, who lines up a little farther from the ball. Typically, nose guards are wide-bodies expected to clog the middle to free teammates to make the tackle.

Bennett, who weighs about 290 pounds, isn't ideal for that job, but he did it willingly.

"I took a more passive approach to nose guard, trying to not make too many mistakes and being as unselfish as possible," Bennett said.

But starting with the Michigan State game, Bennett and Adolphus Washington switched roles to take advantage of Bennett's quickness.

"That's when my game started to (improve), just because of the freedom of playing 3-technique," he said.

Bennett said the coaches were happy with his play at nose guard.

"But they felt I was an unutilized weapon, that I was a guy who could consistently beat single-teams and even

sometimes beat double-teams," he said. "They really wanted to get me in open space, and it's worked out for us."

Bennett credits Washington for making the transition work. Washington was a defensive end who grudgingly moved to tackle before embracing an often-thankless role as the nose guard.

"We understand how each other work and we feed off each other," Bennett said. "Before every game, we say that no one runs through the middle.

"Teams know that if they want to get yards, they have to run outside the tackles. He's learning nose guard and doing a great job."

As the season wore on and the stakes grew, Bennett took on a more vocal leadership role. He chastised his teammates at halftime of the Minnesota game after the Golden Gophers gashed the Buckeyes defense.

He did the same thing during the Michigan game. Both times, his teammates credited him with giving them necessary tough love.

"I feel I have more pride in the off-the-field and team-support things he's done than I have when he sacks the quarterback," Mike Bennett said. "Seeing him pump up the team and take on a leadership role and bring people up around him gives me more of a lasting, enduring sense of pride than some of the stuff he does on the field."

That was especially true in the Big Ten championship game, when Bennett switched from his normal No. 63 to 53 in memory of the late Kosta Karageorge. After each of his tackles, Bennett grabbed his jersey to honor Karageorge.

"I wanted to make sure that if I made a play, people knew that play was for him, and I think the whole team felt that way," Bennett said.

Bennett is a possible first-round pick in May's NFL draft, but that's not something he's dwelling on. All of his efforts are focused on Alabama.

"I live for the games that are absolute battles," he said. "Those are the fun ones." ■

To honor his deceased teammate, Kosta Karageorge, during the Big Ten championship game, Michael Bennett wears jersey No. 53 instead of his usual No. 63. (Adam Cairns/Dispatch)

OHIO STATE 56, RUTGERS 17
October 18, 2014 • Columbus, Ohio

GOOD NIGHT, KNIGHTS

Buckeyes' Train Keeps Rolling Through Big Ten

By Bill Rabinowitz

Can we fast-forward to Nov. 8 already?

Sure, Penn State and Illinois beckon before Ohio State's showdown with Michigan State in East Lansing, and the Buckeyes will no doubt stick to their one-game-at-a-time clichés, as they should.

But No. 13 Ohio State's 56-17 victory over Rutgers was just another hors d'oeuvre that was tasty but hardly filling.

The Scarlet Knights entered the game with a 5-1 record — the loss a close one to Penn State — in their first season as a Big Ten member. But their schedule had been questionable. The Buckeyes exposed them as pretenders.

"Our whole talk all week was that they were a 6-0 team," Meyer said. "That's the way we approached it. I think you can tell by the way our guys came out that there was a lot of respect for that team."

Ohio State (5-1, 2-0) got touchdowns on eight of its first nine drives, with the only empty one coming after a second-quarter possession started with two false-start penalties.

The Buckeyes scored at least 50 points for the fourth straight game, a school record. They have totaled at least 500 yards in each of those games, the first time they have done that in a four-game stretch since 1998.

J.T. Barrett continued his remarkable play as a redshirt freshman quarterback. He passed for 261 yards and three touchdowns and ran for 107 yards and two scores — averaging 15.3 yards a carry. Barrett completed 19 of 31 passes to nine receivers.

Rutgers entered the game tied for third nationally with 24 sacks. But the Scarlet Knights didn't touch Barrett in the pocket until the third quarter, when the game was well under the Buckeyes' control.

"That's the mentality we have for every game, that no one can touch J.T.," right guard Pat Elflein said. "We knew these guys were fast and quick — good pass-rushers. But we were prepared for that and played well."

The Buckeyes defense wasn't as dominating, but it did its part. Ohio State surrendered only one touchdown before the score became lopsided. On Rutgers' third possession, it kept the Buckeyes off-balance on a 66-yard drive that made it 14-7.

After tight end Nick Vannett caught his second touchdown pass to make it 21-7, the defense made the play that ended any doubt about the outcome. After a 53-yard punt by Cameron Johnston pinned Rutgers at its 10, Scarlet Knights quarterback Gary Nova threw a swing pass to Janarion Grant.

The pass was high, forcing Grant to reach to

Tight end Nick Vannett scores a 26-yard touchdown, his second during the 56-17 victory against Rutgers. (Fred Squillante/Dispatch)

snare it, and that gave linebacker Darron Lee time to close on him. Lee grabbed Grant, and defensive end Rashad Frazier arrived to deliver a hit that jarred the ball free. Cornerback Eli Apple scooped up the ball and jogged 4 yards for the score.

On Rutgers' only other good scoring chance in the first half, senior cornerback Doran Grant intercepted a Nova pass in the end zone in the final minute to preserve a 35-7 lead.

Since losing to Virginia Tech in the season's second game, Ohio State has outscored opponents 141-38 in the first half.

"Get out fast and play good pass defense against a team that was on fire throwing the ball," Meyer said of his emphasis before the game. "(Nova is) the most improved quarterback, I think, in the country from a year ago."

Nova completed 17 of 28 passes for 192 yards and was sacked four times.

The second half was a formality. The Buckeyes extended their lead to 56-10 with four minutes left in the third quarter before substituting liberally the rest of the way.

"They have an excellent football team," Rutgers coach Kyle Flood said. "I think today is a great example that when you play a really talented football team, the margin of error is very small. We just didn't play very clean football."

The Buckeyes weren't perfect, either, but they are undeniably a different team than the one that lost to Virginia Tech.

"We're better up front," offensive coordinator Tom Herman said. "We're better at quarterback. We're better at the skill positions.

"The sign of a good team is continual improvement, and I think we're on that track right now."

The train figures to keep rolling, with the big destination coming up in three weeks. ∎

Ohio State players sing *Carmen Ohio* after their 56-17 win over Rutgers. (Adam Cairns/Dispatch)

OHIO STATE 31, PENN STATE 24, 2OT
October 25, 2014 • State College, Pennsylvania

DOUBLE DELIGHT

Ohio State Overcomes Struggles to Win on the Road

By Bill Rabinowitz

For the first time this season, Ohio State played against a credible defense and a truly hostile crowd. It showed.

The Buckeyes squandered a 17-0 halftime lead before prevailing 31-24 in double overtime over Penn State in front of a white-out Beaver Stadium crowd of 107,895.

After Penn State scored on a 1-yard run touchdown run to open overtime, the No. 13 Buckeyes (5-1, 3-0 Big Ten) answered with touchdown runs by quarterback J.T. Barrett of 5 and 4 yards.

The second score was aided by a personal-foul penalty on Penn State linebacker Mike Hull for jumping the pile on the game-tying extra-point kick that ended the first overtime. That let Ohio State start at the Nittany Lions' 12 instead of the 25.

Ohio State then stopped Penn State (4-3, 1-3) on its ensuing possession. On fourth-and-5, Buckeyes defensive end Joey Bosa overpowered running back Akeel Lynch, driving him into Nittany Lions quarterback Christian Hackenberg, who fell, resulting in a game-ending sack.

"When you have as a good a player as Joey Bosa, you probably expect him to make a play in a big situation," coach Urban Meyer said.

The Buckeyes poured onto the field after the sack, more in relief than exhilaration. This was much tougher than they expected against a Penn State team with a patchwork offensive line that had lost its previous two games.

Ohio State, a two-touchdown favorite, had scored 50 points and gained more than 500 yards in its previous four games. But all were against suspect defenses. Penn State was ranked sixth nationally in scoring and total defense and first against the run, though it hadn't played a team with an offense nearly as potent as Ohio State's.

The Nittany Lions got the better of the matchup in regulation. The Buckeyes gained only 293 yards, including only 80 in the second half. Until the overtime, Barrett resembled the redshirt freshman he looked like in the loss to Virginia Tech more than the polished, poised player he had been lately. Meyer said Barrett played with a sprained knee in the second half.

With the play-calling unusually conservative, Barrett passed for only 74 yards. The Buckeyes seldom tested Penn State's secondary deep and were often content to run between the tackles. It worked early, but wasn't sustained.

Ohio State's only possession deep in Penn State territory in the final 30 minutes of regulation ended on a missed 41-yard field-goal attempt by Sean Nuernberger in the third quarter.

When OSU did turn to the air, the results were sometimes disastrous. Penn State defensive tackle

Defensive back Vonn Bell (11) celebrates his controversial first-quarter interception. (Chris Russell/Dispatch)

Anthony Zettel intercepted Barrett and returned the ball 40 yards for a touchdown on the Buckeyes' first possession of the second half to begin the Nittany Lions' comeback.

Barrett was picked off again early in the fourth quarter when he was off-target to Evan Spencer, and Hull caught the ball. The Nittany Lions drove 60 yards, the final 24 coming on a touchdown pass from Hackenberg to Saeed Blacknall, who outleaped Eli Apple for the ball to make the score 17-14.

Penn State then tied the score on a 19-play drive that ended with a 31-yard field goal by Sam Ficken with nine seconds left.

When Penn State scored on a 1-yard run by Bill Belton after the Nittany Lions overcame a holding call on their first play of overtime, the Buckeyes looked to be in deep trouble.

But the offense awoke from its slumber just in time. Barrett ran 17 yards on a keeper, and then scored on the next play for a tie.

Ohio State got the ball first in double overtime. After a 2-yard run by sophomore running back Ezekiel Elliott, Barrett scrambled for 6 yards and then bulled in for the final 4.

Then the Buckeyes' defense did what it couldn't do in the fourth quarter: shut Penn State down when it needed to.

The Buckeyes caught breaks from the officiating on their first two scores. On Penn State's game-opening possession, safety Vonn Bell was credited with an interception, though replays showed the ball touched the ground. Later, it was announced that the replay officials got the wrong feed from ABC. OSU made it 10-0 on a 49-yard field goal by Nuernberger on which the referees did not notice that the play clock had expired.

Penn State coach James Franklin said: "I'd love to come in here and tell you how I really think, but that would be inappropriate with some of the other things that went on." ∎

Defensive lineman Joey Bosa sacks Penn State quarterback Christian Hackenberg on fourth and 5 in the second overtime to seal Ohio State's victory. (Brooke LaValley/Dispatch)

Michael Bennett (63), Joey Bosa (97) and Ezekiel Elliott (15) celebrate the Buckeyes' overtime win against Penn State with the singing of *Carmen Ohio*. (Chris Russell/Dispatch)

• WIDE RECEIVER •

EVAN SPENCER

Stats Don't Tell the Whole Story for Unselfish Senior

By Bill Rabinowitz • October 25, 2014

Two highlight-reel catches bookend Evan Spencer's career at Ohio State.

In his first college game, as a freshman in 2011, Spencer made a leaping, one-handed sideline reception of a Braxton Miller pass against Akron.

Against Rutgers, Spencer capped Ohio State's 56-17 victory by stretching to make a one-handed catch of a J.T. Barrett toss, this time for a touchdown. Spencer has practiced hard to make those kinds of spectacular catches, but those plays miss the essence of what the senior has meant to the Buckeyes. Spencer's calling card is the grunt work that usually goes unnoticed by outsiders.

Spencer has only seven catches this season, for 73 yards and two touchdowns. Those usually are numbers that get a starting wide receiver benched. Not in Spencer's case.

His relentless blocking, special-teams contributions and leadership have given him prominent status inside the Woody Hayes Athletic Center.

"It's hard for me to say he's not one of our MVPs, the way he's playing for us," Ohio State coach Urban Meyer said.

• • • • • • • •

College players often talk about their deep love of their school. Evan Spencer comes by his honestly.

"I probably came out of the womb wearing a Buckeye helmet," he said.

His father, Tim, was a star running back for the Buckeyes from 1979 to '82. After an eight-year pro career, Tim Spencer returned to Ohio State for 10 years as running backs coach. He has the same position now with the Tampa Bay Buccaneers.

As a kid, Evan loved nothing more than tagging along to Buckeyes practices with his dad and hanging around with the players he watched on Saturdays.

"I was always bouncing off the walls and needed to be doing something," Spencer said. "I had a lot of energy and still kind of do. That's my personality."

One time, when he was about 8 or 9, he couldn't resist the urge and joined the huddle during practice, much to the amusement of the players (and probably not as much of his father).

Even when the Spencers moved to Chicago after Tim got a job coaching the Bears' running backs, Evan never lost his passion for the Buckeyes. Although he was open-minded during the recruiting process, his decision to return to Columbus surprised no one.

When he made that catch against Akron in 2011, it looked as if he might develop into a receiver who would put up big numbers. It hasn't worked out that way, partly because of injuries, partly because Ohio State's passing game was inconsistent, and now because he is part of a deep receiver rotation.

Wide receiver Evan Spencer makes one of his two catches against Navy. (Eamon Queeney/Dispatch)

Would he like to catch the ball more? Of course. But he embraces the requirement that his job is more than catching the football. Spencer also is a leader on coverage units in the kicking game.

"I really pride myself on being a complete football player," Spencer said. "I've never been a selfish-type person. Obviously, you have to be a selfish person, to an extent, in sports to be successful. But I've always been a team player.

"I'm going to do whatever I have to do, or is needed of me to do, to win the game. If that means catch a 70-yard touchdown pass, I'll do that. If it means to secure the edge (with a block) so we can get the running backs on the edge and have a perimeter run game, it's part of the job description."

Receivers coach Zach Smith described Spencer's blocking as "phenomenal." That's why he's not obsessed with his skimpy receiving statistics.

"He's not a guy who lights up the stats sheet, because they keep stats on catches and yards (only)," Smith said. "In the film room, he lights the film up. Opponents know who he is and think he is a really good player. Maybe the media or the national news doesn't, because all they care about is touchdowns and catches.

"He is one of the better players I've ever coached. His respect is as high as it can be around here."

Redshirt freshman Jalin Marshall even called Spencer the "class president" of the receivers group.

Such is the respect for Spencer that Meyer last week did what he seldom does — design plays specifically to get the ball to him. Almost always, Meyer and offensive coordinator Tom Herman insist that no specific receiver is targeted on any pass play. The quarterback throws to the best option based on what he sees from the coverage.

But after Barrett and Spencer failed to connect several times earlier in the Rutgers game, Meyer wanted Spencer to get some glory. That's how he ended up with the chance to make the one-handed touchdown grab.

"I just trust him with everything," Meyer said. "It's to the point that we're trying to find ways to reward him. That (is why) we threw to him three times in the red zone. That was all me trying to reward a person who is selfless. I just love who he is right now."

Spencer is on track to graduate in December with a degree in economics. He is taking a course load filled with, as he jokes, "crazy 5,000-level" classes. But academics are serious business with the Spencers. His mother, Gilda, is a senior vice president and deputy general counsel for Allstate.

He is as much his mother's son as his father's.

"I think she's the best mom in the world," Spencer said. "She has always been there for me, and at the same time, she has been successful on her own career path. That has given me motivation."

Spencer has NFL aspirations, so he hopes this will not be his final year of football. But his experience at Ohio State, he said, has been everything he hoped.

"Being able to play football at Ohio State was one of the goals I set when I was probably 3 years old," Spencer said. "Being able to play here, be successful here and being able to start here is every dream that I probably ever had.

"Obviously, I've got more to play at the next level. But at least one of my dreams was checked off the list — being able to play here and put Evan's stamp on the Spencer name here at Ohio State." ■

Evan Spencer's meager numbers aren't what make him such an important Ohio State wide receiver — his blocking, special-teams contributions and leadership are. (Kyle Robertson/Dispatch)

OHIO STATE 55, ILLINOIS 14
November 1, 2014 • Columbus, Ohio

BUCKEYES ROMP

Ohio State Wins 20th Straight Regular-Season Big Ten Contest

By Bill Rabinowitz

All week, Ohio State's players and coaches insisted they would not look past Illinois toward next week's showdown against Michigan State.

They were true to their word. The No. 13 Buckeyes got more help than resistance from their opponent, Illinois, rolling to a 55-14 victory at Ohio Stadium.

Ohio State's defense caused four turnovers, three of which were converted into scores.

"I thought our defense came out and played really well," Buckeyes coach Urban Meyer said.

Quarterback J.T. Barrett, who suffered a sprained knee ligament in last week's double-overtime victory over Penn State, showed no ill effects from the injury in one half of work.

"The knee really didn't give me any problems," Barrett said.

The victory was the 20th straight regular-season Big Ten victory for Ohio State, tying the conference record set by the 2005-07 Buckeyes. No. 21 will not come as easily. The Buckeyes and Spartans have seemingly been on a collision course since Michigan State ended Ohio State's 24-game winning streak under Meyer in last year's Big Ten championship game.

"We've not talked about it much," Meyer said. "Obviously, the dream was ripped away from us by a very good team."

The Spartans had a bye this week. The Buckeyes (7-1, 4-0 Big Ten) might as well have,

given how overmatched and mistake-prone the Illini were. There's a reason that Illinois (4-5, 1-4) has won only two league games in three seasons under Tim Beckman.

One came last week against once-beaten Minnesota. That got their attention, and the Buckeyes played as if focused on the here and now.

Ohio State led 31-0 at halftime, and it probably should have been worse. Twice, the Buckeyes were stopped on fourth down deep inside Illinois territory, the second time on fourth-and-goal from the 1.

The closest Illinois came to scoring in the first half came when Beckman passed up a chance to kick a field goal on fourth-and-2 from the Ohio State 12 in the second quarter with the Buckeyes ahead 24-0. Defensive end Joey Bosa threw down backup Illinois quarterback Aaron Bailey for a loss on a bootleg.

Earlier, the Illini missed a 47-yard field-goal attempt.

The Buckeyes' defense did more than stop Illinois. Linebackers Darron Lee and Curtis Grant had interceptions off of deflections thrown by starter Reilly O'Toole. Safety Tyvis Powell caused a fumble on a crunching hit on running back Josh Ferguson.

Lee's interception and 26-yard return on Illinois' opening possession set up Ohio State's first score. Freshman running back Curtis Samuel, who earned the start over Ezekiel Elliott with a strong week of practice, scored on a 23-yard run.

Running back Dontre Wilson catches a touchdown pass, one of his two receptions in the third quarter against Illinois. (Chris Russell/Dispatch)

Grant's interception gave the ball to Ohio State at the Illinois 24 and set up Samuel's second score on a 1-yard run.

Barrett wasn't sharp early, overthrowing some receivers, but he settled in. He finished 15 of 24 for 167 yards and two touchdowns, both to Devin Smith. He also ran seven times for 38 yards before becoming a spectator for the entire second half.

Smith's first touchdown came on a 32-yarder in which he beat cornerback Darius Mosely and made a nifty over-the-shoulder catch on Barrett's perfect throw.

If there was to be any suspense about the second half, Smith ended it with his second score, which was aided by a questionable decision by Beckman.

After the Illini stopped Elliott on a shovel pass on fourth-and-goal, Illinois took over at its 2 with 1:38 left. On second down, Illinois attempted a short sideline pass, which fell incomplete. That allowed Ohio State to use its only remaining timeout after a third-down run.

The Buckeyes got a 28-yard punt return by Jalin Marshall to take over at the Illinois 25 with 34 seconds left. The Buckeyes needed only two plays to score — a 17-yard pass to Dontre Wilson and then Smith's 8-yard touchdown catch to make it 31-0.

Backup quarterback Cardale Jones threw 27 yards to Wilson on Ohio State's opening drive of the third quarter to extend the lead to 38-0.

By then, the only drama was whether the Buckeyes could maintain the shutout. That bid ended with mostly Ohio State backups on the field late in the third quarter when Donovonn Young capped a 65-yard drive with a 5-yard touchdown run to make it 48-7. ∎

Running back Curtis Samuel, who had nine carries, 63 yards and two touchdowns, breaks the barrier for a touchdown in the second quarter. (Eamon Queeney/Dispatch)

OHIO STATE 49, MICHIGAN STATE 37
November 8, 2014 • East Lansing, Michigan

SIGNATURE VICTORY

In His Third Season, Urban Meyer Finally Beats Top 10 Opponent

By Bill Rabinowitz

In three seasons under coach Urban Meyer, the Ohio State football team has lacked only one thing — a signature victory over a top-10 team.

Not anymore.

Ohio State gained the inside track for a spot in the Big Ten championship game and kept afloat its hopes for the College Football Playoff with a 49-37 victory last night over No. 7 Michigan State at Spartan Stadium.

"This is one for the ages," Meyer said. "That's how much respect we had for our opponent."

The 14th-ranked Buckeyes (8-1, 5-0 Big Ten) won their 21st straight regular-season conference game, a league record. More important, they avenged a loss to Michigan State in last year's league title game. That first defeat of Meyer's Buckeyes kept Ohio State out of last year's national championship game.

This Ohio State team has a much different cast, but even those players who watched on the sideline or their couches that night were hungry to help reassert the Buckeyes' supremacy in the Big Ten.

They were up to the challenge. After trailing 21-14, the Buckeyes' offense got touchdowns on its next six possessions against a defense that ranked fifth nationally in total yards allowed. Ohio State gained 568 yards.

In Ohio State's two previous games against credible defenses — Virginia Tech and Penn State —

redshirt freshman quarterback J.T. Barrett had thrown five of his seven interceptions.

He played flawlessly against the Spartans. He didn't commit a turnover and completed 16 of 26 passes for 300 yards, with 129 of them going to Devin Smith.

"We had to answer each one of their hits and we did," Meyer said. "He was very accurate on the deep balls. Devin Smith, that's his best game in the last three years."

Barrett ran for 86 yards, including a 55-yard dash to set up a score that all but clinched the game with seven minutes left.

Ezekiel Elliott ran for 154 yards and two touchdowns behind an offensive line that consistently opened holes.

The defense rallied after a shaky start. Michigan State (7-2, 4-1) got touchdowns on three of its first five possessions. Ohio State held the Spartans to only one field goal in their next five drives as the Buckeyes asserted control.

"I'm very proud of our guys," Meyer said. "A young team grew up tonight. I told them that the future is extremely bright at Ohio State."

The first half was marked by sudden momentum shifts and offenses that were seldom stopped, except by themselves.

Ohio State overcame two special-teams turnovers

Wide receiver Devin Smith catches a touchdown pass, one of his six receptions, in the second quarter against Michigan State. (Adam Cairns/Dispatch)

"THIS IS A DIFFERENT BUCKEYE TEAM THAN IT WAS EARLY IN THE SEASON. THIS TEAM RIGHT NOW IS PLAYING ON A VERY, VERY HIGH LEVEL."
— URBAN MEYER

Devin Smith races past Michigan State linebacker Riley Bullough during the first quarter.
(Kyle Robertson/Dispatch)

and a missed 47-yard field-goal attempt to lead 28-21.

After Michigan State needed only five plays to go 63 yards to take a 7-0 lead, the Buckeyes answered with an even quicker score set up by a 47-yard run by Ezekiel Elliott.

Michigan State then took advantage of the first major mistake of the game. After the Buckeyes forced a punt, Jeff Greene could not get out of the way of a short kick. The ball hit him and the Spartans recovered. On the next play, Jeremy Langford ran 33 yards for a touchdown.

A hands-to-the-face penalty on Taylor Decker wiped out a first down at MSU's 9 on OSU's next possession, and the Buckeyes eventually had to punt on fourth-and-45.

The Buckeyes tied it when Barrett scored on a fourth-and-goal keeper at the 1 before Michigan State drove 66 yards in 14 plays to go ahead 21-14.

When Dontre Wilson fumbled on the ensuing kickoff return at Ohio State's 18, the Buckeyes looked to be in serious trouble. But a touchdown run was wiped out on a holding call, and Michael Geiger missed a 39-yard field-goal try.

That proved to be the turning point as Ohio State took the lead with two big plays.

First, Michael Thomas caught a pass on a slant, shed a tackle by cornerback Darian Hicks and scored on a 79-yard catch.

The Buckeyes went ahead 28-21 on a beautiful 44-yard touchdown catch by Smith with 56 seconds left before halftime.

"This is a different Buckeye team than it was early in the season," Meyer said. "This team right now is playing on a very, very high level." ■

Wide receiver Michael Thomas escapes a tackle on his way to a 79-yard touchdown during the second quarter. (Adam Cairns/Dispatch)

97

• DEFENSIVE LINEMAN •

JOEY BOSA

Bosa Knew From an Early Age that Defensive End Was His Position

By Tim May • November 15, 2014

Just as every baseball power hitter probably remembers his first home run, almost every extraordinary pass-rushing defensive end is likely to recall his first sack.

But for Joey Bosa, it took a while to summon the image. Ohio State's sophomore defensive end had to dig through his pee-wee football memories to find it.

After all, he started his football life as a 6-year-old quarterback.

"Every little kid starts playing quarterback, and so did I, in Pembroke Pines (Fla.)," Bosa said. "Then I started getting bigger, and I wasn't the best quarterback."

A cursory study of his DNA would have forecast his eventual move to defense. His father, John, was a star defensive end at Boston College and a first-round draft pick of the Miami Dolphins in 1987. His uncle, Eric Kumerow, was a standout defensive end at Ohio State and a first-round pick of the Dolphins in 1988.

"I loved going to D-line," Joey Bosa said. "I felt like I was following my dad and playing his position. I wasn't a quarterback. I always thought I could play it (if needed), but it's more fun hitting people than throwing the ball."

He snickered. The main thing he wanted to avoid was being the big kid typecast as an overall lineman.

"I didn't mind D-end as long as I didn't have to play offensive line," he said. He was tried at both for a while — including with the Pembroke Pines Bengals — "but I always acted like I hated O-line so much, because I did."

Bosa had a simple answer as to why he wanted nothing to do with the offensive line: "I thought it was boring. That's about it."

"I guess I'm just a D-lineman at heart," he said, "because I can't really stand the O-linemen.

"I mean, our guys, my teammates, I love them off the field, but on the field we just can't be friends. I mean, they're trying to block you. You've got to have a little bit of hate for them deep down."

Even as he closes in on Vernon Gholston's OSU record of 14 sacks in a season, set in 2007, Bosa had to think before he remembered the first time he landed the grand prize for a pass-rusher.

"It was my second year playing (in pee-wee ball), and they had moved me to D-end because we had another quarterback," he said. "I just remember that first game playing it and everyone was like, 'Oh, that's his spot.'

"I tried moving to outside linebacker in high school (at the heralded St. Thomas Aquinas program in Fort Lauderdale), but when they moved me back down to the D-line, it was a natural fit. Just knew it."

Although he couldn't pinpoint his first sack right

Sophomore defensive lineman Joey Bosa tackles Wisconsin Badgers running back Melvin Gordon, who accumulated 2,587 yards this season. Bosa realized early on that defense was a natural fit for him. (Kyle Robertson/Dispatch)

away, he did know how he felt. He said it's the same feeling he gets now when he brings down the quarterback, then jumps up and does his signature shrug.

"It's almost like a relief because you go into a game wondering, 'Am I going to make a play? Am I going to play well?'" Bosa said. "Then, when you hit someone, when you get a sack, there's a release of emotion and you feel more relaxed. And once you make a play, you just keep playing better and building on it."

That's why he knew defensive end was his position — and was aware of it before anyone else.

"It's hard to explain sometimes when something feels so natural," Bosa said. "Like at outside linebacker, I didn't like standing up like that all the time. I never got used to it. I didn't even make the JV team my freshman year. Then they moved me to D-line, and all the coaches were freaking out about the way I got off the ball. I don't know, I just had a knack for it, I guess."

Now in his second season of college football, he has added technique to his natural ability. Observers have noticed.

"Joey Bosa is, I think, the best defensive-front player in all of college football this year," ESPN analyst Todd McShay said this week.

Jerry Kill didn't offer an argument against that notion. As Minnesota's coach, he has studied the video in anticipation of today's game with the Buckeyes, and he has seen the same things in Bosa that McShay has.

"He's a big-time player," Kill said. "He's going to play at the next level. Like our (offensive coaches) have said, you're playing against an NFL defensive end.

"He gets off the ball quick. He uses his hands very well. He is hard to maintain a block on. And he's just a very good athlete, born with some instincts. He's NFL-ready right now, so that's a big challenge for us."

Penn State coach James Franklin saw those things in action against his offense. Bosa had two sacks that night in a hard-fought, double-overtime victory by the Buckeyes. He also delivered his most memorable play to date, a bull rush into Nittany Lions running back Akeel

Lynch, who had stayed in the backfield to help block on a fourth-down pass. Bosa, though, drove Lynch straight back into quarterback Christian Hackenberg, who folded to the ground, ending the game in the second overtime.

"Really good player, real strong, real big, real physical," Franklin said of Bosa. "Typically, you have defensive ends who are undersized and athletic, quick and fast. And you have big guys that are physical in the run game. He's got a combination of both."

So why was a player who leads the Big Ten with 10 sacks feeling so frustrated after the Buckeyes' victory at Michigan State last week? The Spartans were determined to keep him off the sack board, and they did.

"I respect it, definitely, how teams have been game-planning against me," Bosa said. "I'm happy with that. That's respecting me, which obviously any player wants to earn, and it helps free up my teammates who work just as hard as I do every day (and) gives them a chance to shine.

"I just want more from myself every single time I play. It's not that I'm upset selfishly that I didn't do well. It's that I'm upset that I couldn't have done more to help the team overall."

But the Michigan State game also offered more examples of how Ohio State defensive coordinators Luke Fickell and Chris Ash are trying to set up Bosa for more favorable matchups. Fickell and Ash have been moving Bosa inside at times in pass-rush situations, occasionally having him stand behind defensive tackle Michael Bennett before the snap, then picking his spot.

In a perfect world, Bosa would prefer working from just one spot — defensive end — and honing his craft. But he appreciates being the wild card, too.

"It's fun to mix it up," he said.

Just as long as no one gets the bright idea of moving him to the offensive line. ∎

Joey Bosa hugs coach Urban Meyer during the fourth quarter of the Big Ten championship game. (Adam Cairns/Dispatch)

OHIO STATE 31, MINNESOTA 24
November 15, 2014 • Minneapolis, Minnesota

FROZEN TREAT

J.T. Barrett Rushes for 189 Yards During Frigid Contest

By Bill Rabinowitz

The weather was the coldest for an Ohio State game in at least 50 years, with the added fun of constant snow.

At times, the Buckeyes were their own worst enemy.

Their opponent, though limited by a meager passing game, was every bit the well-drilled team they expected, and it took advantage of those mistakes. So even though a 31-24 victory over Minnesota at TCF Bank Stadium was closer than it should have been at a time of year when style points matter, Ohio State was in no mood to apologize.

"This is a tough environment," coach Urban Meyer said. "I'd like to see any team in the country come up here and do this — play here in November against a very good team. Have at it."

This had all the elements of a trap game — an emotional win over Michigan State last week, a kickoff at 11 a.m. local time after three straight night games, 15 degrees at kickoff and an up-and-coming opponent eager to stake its claim as a bona fide Big Ten contender.

"The whole deal made it potential for an upset," offensive line coach Ed Warinner said. "We did everything we could to prepare and educate the players."

They started as if they had gotten the message, even if the weather was frightful.

"When everybody first came out — the running backs, the offensive line — everybody was like, 'It's going to be a long day' because of the cold weather," defensive tackle Adolphus Washington said. "But once everyone started playing, it was like the weather didn't really exist."

Sparked by J.T. Barrett's 86-yard touchdown run — the longest ever by an Ohio State quarterback — eighth-ranked Ohio State jumped to a 14-0 lead late in the first quarter.

After that, though, the game morphed into a competition in which Ohio State's statistical dominance was undermined by costly mistakes. Even with a passing game that often misfired in the frigid conditions, the Buckeyes (9-1, 6-0 Big Ten) outgained the Golden Gophers 489-303.

Barrett finished with 189 yards on 17 carries to set a record for most rushing yards in a game by an Ohio State quarterback.

But the Buckeyes committed three turnovers, all of which the Gophers (7-3, 4-2) converted into touchdowns.

The momentum first flipped when Brian Boddy-Calhoun intercepted Barrett's off-target deep pass to Corey Smith and returned it 56 yards to the Ohio State 39-yard line.

Minnesota's offense, held without a first down on its first three possessions, then came alive. Proving to be every bit the beast that Ohio State feared, running back David Cobb (27 carries for 145 yards) ran five

Quarterback J.T. Barrett leaves the Gophers defense in the dust as he races for the Buckeyes' first touchdown against Minnesota. (Chris Russell/Dispatch)

straight times to give the Gophers their first touchdown.

The Buckeyes were on the verge of taking a 21-7 lead when they drove to the Minnesota 7, only to see Jalin Marshall fumble and the Gophers recover the ball in the end zone. Six minutes and 80 yards later, Minnesota tied the score. On third-and-15, Cobb slipped an attempted tackle by safety Tyvis Powell on a 30-yard scoring run.

Touchdown catches by Michael Thomas on a busted coverage and Evan Spencer on a screen play gave the Buckeyes a 31-14 lead with 10 minutes left.

When Ohio State forced a punt on Minnesota's next possession, the game seemed in hand. But Marshall dropped a fair catch, and Minnesota recovered. Cobb's 12-yard run made it 31-21.

The Gophers kicked a field goal to cut Ohio State's lead to seven with 1:19 left, but Ohio State's Jeff Heuerman recovered the Gophers' onside kick to secure the victory.

"Great team win," Meyer said. "Not great execution, but a great team win."

Added offensive coordinator Tom Herman, "This was a top-25 team (in the College Football Playoff rankings) with a top-20 defense. (We were) on the road with very unfavorable conditions and we turned the ball over (three) times and still found a way to win.

"So it's a great team effort and very encouraging. But obviously we're not going to be able to go where we want to go turning the ball over like that." ■

Defensive lineman Adolphus Washington (high) and linebacker Joshua Perry (low) bring down Minnesota quarterback Mitch Leidner in the third quarter. (Kyle Robertson/Dispatch)

Ohio State players celebrate the road victory with their fans while singing *Carmen Ohio*. (Kyle Robertson/Dispatch)

SLICK MOVES

Buckeyes Shake Off Turnovers to Clinch Division Title

By Bill Rabinowitz

Some of them tried to put a pleasant face on it.

It was a 15-point victory. It did clinch the Big Ten East division title for Ohio State and a return trip to the conference championship game. No Buckeye suffered a serious injury.

But to call Ohio State's 42-27 victory over visiting Indiana yesterday anything but lackluster is an exercise in spin control.

"I'm not happy about the win," safety Tyvis Powell said. "A win is a win in the books, but everybody in the locker room feels sick about the win. We know we have room to get better, and that's what we need to do, especially since we have the rivalry game coming up" against Michigan on Saturday.

The scare against a Hoosiers team that was winless in the Big Ten and a five-touchdown underdog isn't a mortal blow to the Buckeyes' standing in the College Football Playoff rankings, but it won't help. Ohio State is sixth and needs to move to fourth in the next two weeks to earn a spot in the national semifinals.

And if not for Jalin Marshall's huge bounce-back performance, Ohio State might have been looking at a disaster.

A week after losing two key fumbles at Minnesota, Marshall scored four straight touch-downs, starting with a 54-yard punt return that erased a 20-14 third-quarter Indiana lead.

"There's definitely a little bit of redemption," the redshirt freshman said. "I'm just satisfied with the team win. I feel like that was very important to the win today, so I'm excited about that."

As was the case last week, Ohio State (10-1, 7-0 Big Ten) took a 14-0 lead and looked headed for a rout. As was the case last week, the Buckeyes committed three turnovers — a fumble by receiver Michael Thomas and two interceptions thrown by J.T. Barrett — to give their opponent oxygen.

The differences were that Indiana (3-8, 0-7) isn't as good as Minnesota and that it took Ohio State's offense a while to escape the doldrums even after the string of turnovers ended.

"We jumped out to a 14-0 lead, and the stadium was dead, and we were dead," coach Urban Meyer said.

The fans had an excuse. Icy roads caused many in the announced crowd of 101,426 at Ohio Stadium to arrive late.

Tardy fans missed a 65-yard touchdown run by Ezekiel Elliott and a 4-yard touchdown pass from Barrett to Jeff Heuerman on Ohio State's first two drives.

But Indiana scored after a 53-yard scramble by freshman quarterback Zander Diamont on third-and-11, and then came the Buckeyes' three consecutive turnovers, followed by four straight punts.

Freshman running back Jalin Marshall runs untouched into the end zone in the fourth quarter against Indiana. Marshall dominated the second half with four touchdowns. (Chris Russell/Dispatch)

"That's just what turnovers do," Elliott said. "Turnovers are momentum-swingers. We lost all our momentum with the turnovers."

Ohio State held Indiana star running back Tevin Coleman in check in the first half. But midway through the third quarter, he ran 90 yards untouched to put Indiana ahead 20-14.

Then Marshall took over. Buckeyes punter Cameron Johnston pinned the Hoosiers at their 1-yard line with a 50-yard line drive that somehow died before it would have rolled into the end zone. Ohio State's defense forced a three-and-out, and Marshall caught the punt, headed upfield, made one sharp cut and went untouched into the end zone.

Marshall then caught three touchdown passes — two on shovel passes to allow Barrett to break Troy Smith's Ohio State record for touchdown passes in a season — as the Buckeyes pulled away late.

Coleman's 52-yard touchdown with just over a minute left gave him 228 yards in the game.

"Sometimes in college football, things don't go exactly as scripted," Meyer said.

"We're fine. It was somewhat of a close call. We just have to play better, but we still are division champs."

Still, it's the second straight close call at a time when it's important to be peaking.

"It's icy, and the stadium's not full at the beginning of the game, and you're playing a team that's 0-6 in the Big Ten," Heuerman said. "The juice level is kind of down.

"It was just kind of one of those games, but we battled through it and got the win, and that's all that matters."

Now it's on to Michigan. Even though the Wolverines are having another forgettable season, the rivalry still is the rivalry.

"Regardless of records or anything, the most motivated, most prepared team will win this next game," Meyer said. "That's this rivalry." ∎

Safety Tyvis Powell returns an interception in the fourth quarter against Indiana. (Eamon Queeney/Dispatch)

SENIOR CLASS

From Bans to Bowl Games, the 24 OSU Seniors Have Seen It All
By Tim May • November 29, 2014

As tradition dictates, the Ohio State seniors will be introduced one at a time before the 111th game with Michigan, and they will stride onto the field with a rose in hand but, to hear them tell it, a void in their competitive hearts.

In their four years — or five, in the case of right tackle Darryl Baldwin — they have endured one of the few scandals and brief depressions in the program's history, only to rise to be part of the longest winning streak in school history (24 games), as well as the longest Big Ten winning streak in regular-season games, which is at 23 and counting.

But something more meaningful is missing.

"We've been through a lot, but we don't have any of those championships, I guess you could say," tight end Jeff Heuerman said. "The first year (2011) we lost the Gator Bowl, the second year we were ineligible (to play in the postseason), then last year we lost the Big Ten championship (and the Orange Bowl).

"So as a senior, we just want to go out with a championship. That's something my class doesn't have to put next to our name."

It has been a point of conversation for a while among the players in the outgoing class which, including walk-ons, numbers 24.

"We just sat back and really talked to each other, the guys in our class, 'We haven't won anything since we've been here,'" cornerback Doran Grant said. "We won a couple of division championships (actually three), but we haven't won a Big Ten title since I've been here. So that's our main goal, to win this Big Ten championship and, of course, beat the team up north."

The latter goal comes before the former. But regardless of what happens against rival Michigan, the Buckeyes already have clinched the Big Ten East Division title and a second straight trip to the Big Ten title game in Indianapolis.

"It basically fires us up because we don't want to be that class that doesn't win anything," Grant said. "We know how important this is to us, personally, and also to the team and to the fans. … We want to win the top prize."

That's one reason that coach Urban Meyer said the jury is still out on the 2014 seniors, a group made up predominantly of members from the 2011 recruiting class he inherited when he took the job at the end of the 2011 season. That class has dwindled from 23 players on signing day to the 10 who will take their final bow today, plus four who are fourth-year juniors and one (backup quarterback Cardale Jones) who is a third-year sophomore.

There is no doubt the 2014 seniors have been part of some great runs, Meyer said, but in terms of leadership and pushing a team to greatness, "This book isn't written yet. So I'm pleased with it. But these next couple (of games) are going to — that is going to be their legacy; our legacy, I should say."

Defensive tackle Michael Bennett understands the

Senior defensive tackle Michael Bennett elevates to try to bat down a pass by Michigan quarterback Devin Gardner. (Chris Russell/Dispatch)

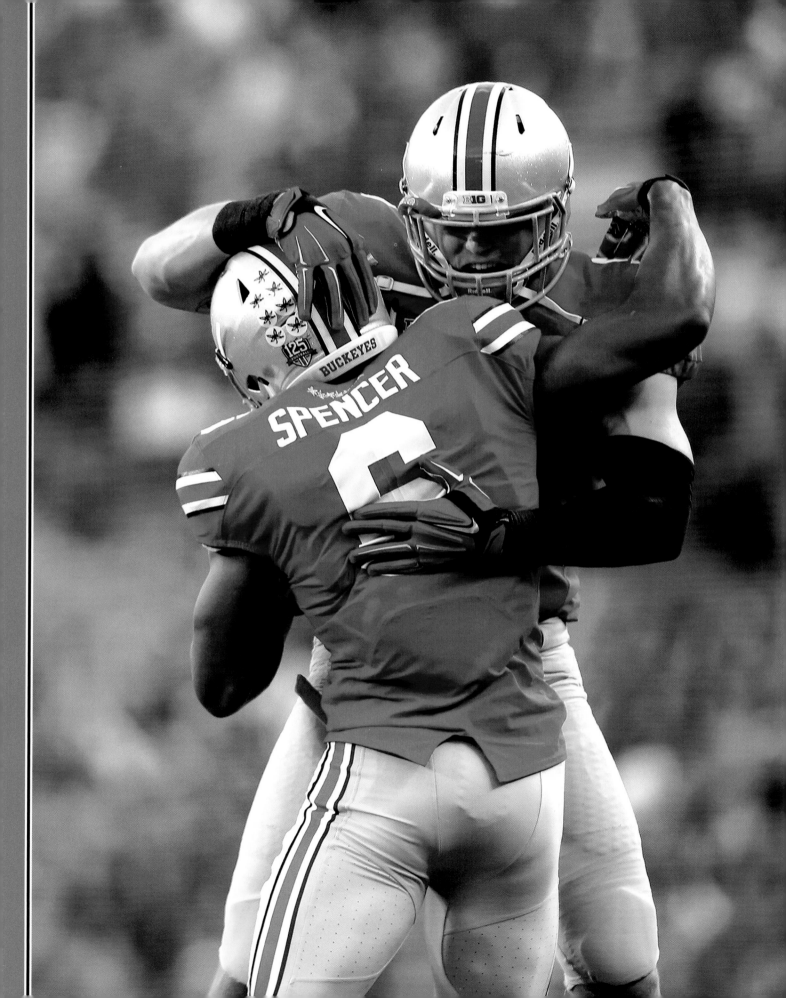

expectations. He knows the Buckeyes not only are in the running for a Big Ten title, but also are sitting No. 6 in the College Football Playoff rankings, with a shot of making the first four-team playoff field if they take care of business these next two games.

"It would be very important as leaders to rally a lot of these young players who have been contributing, and then all of the older players, and come out on top with a Big Ten championship, and maybe more," Bennett said.

Regardless of what happens down the stretch, junior linebacker Joshua Perry said the seniors have made their mark with their younger teammates.

"They care a lot about the team, they care a lot about each other, and they care a lot about helping guys develop and grow as people," Perry said. "That's one of the coolest things I've seen from the people we have as seniors right now, a lot of them are really selfless guys and they've been through a lot of the bad times here, so they know to help the other guys out. They want to make sure other guys can be in positions where they can be successful."

The only scholarship senior who has really seen it all is Baldwin. His first year in the program the Buckeyes won the Big Ten title and went to the Sugar Bowl, where they beat Arkansas. Of course, none of that is in the record book anymore, after OSU vacated its victories from the 2010 season in the aftermath of the tattoos-for-memorabilia scandal and other NCAA violations that cost coach Jim Tressel his job in May 2011.

Tressel was replaced on an interim basis by Luke Fickell, and a tumultuous 2011 season followed. Meyer then came aboard.

"It absolutely was a roller coaster, especially losing Coach Tressel the way we did, and then Coach Fickell having to step up, and then Coach Meyer getting here," Baldwin said. "The time it took to get used to it all — we're still getting used to it, I think. It was an adjustment, and I think we adapted to it pretty well."

What he and today's fourth-year seniors did was help the Buckeyes climb from the abyss of the 2011 season and NCAA sanctions.

"Coach Meyer, when he came in here, he made it very clear that that wasn't going to happen again," Bennett said. "And it hasn't. So I never really thought we were going to go back to that. I still don't. Now it's time to take it to the next level and stop winning just regular-season games and start winning postseason games."

Receiver Evan Spencer agreed.

"We've shown the ability to endure everything we had to go through, and thriving in what we could do in 2012, that first season under Coach Meyer," Spencer said. "We couldn't go to a bowl so we said, 'We're going to do everything we can to go undefeated this year,' to kind of put that statement to the world, 'Hey, we can't go to a bowl this year, but we're still not going to lose.'

"Then last year, going 12-0 again and getting to the Big Ten championship game, we've taken steps. I feel we persevered very well."

But he also said the seniors want to take those next couple of steps to the top of the ladder before bidding OSU adieu. He'll clutch that rose today, but he wants hardware.

"That's why the one goal I put for myself was to play as hard as I possibly can this year," Spencer said. "The reason being, I don't have any of those kinds of wins and I want to make sure I do everything I can to get one." ■

Tight end Jeff Heuerman leaps to congratulate fellow senior Evan Spencer after the wide receiver scores a touchdown against Cincinnati. (Adam Cairns/Dispatch)

OHIO STATE 42, MICHIGAN 28
November 29, 2014 • Columbus, Ohio

A BIG LOSS IN A BIG WIN

Barrett Fractures Ankle Against Rival, Clouds OSU's Prospects

By Bill Rabinowitz

J.T. Barrett lay on the ground, his season over and Ohio State's victory over a supposedly overmatched Michigan team far from certain.

As one Buckeyes teammate after another gave him a consoling slap of hands, the quarterback's message was clear.

"He said, 'Win this game,'" senior tight end Jeff Heuerman said. "He said that it's not about him, it's about us."

It will have to be now. Despite Barrett's injury, a broken right ankle, on the first play of the fourth quarter, Ohio State pulled away for a 42-28 victory at Ohio Stadium over its stubborn rival to become the first team in Big Ten history to win all of its conference regular-season games for three straight seasons.

But the Buckeyes (11-1, 8-0) now must rely on their third-string quarterback, third-year sophomore Cardale Jones, in the Big Ten championship game on Saturday against Wisconsin and beyond.

Heuerman acknowledged that Barrett's injury tempered the unbridled joy that is supposed to result from beating Michigan.

"It's tough, especially walking off that field for the last time and knowing the guy you've rallied around all season is hurt," Heuerman said. "But you've got to keep moving forward."

The Buckeyes can take strength from knowing that they did exactly that after Barrett's injury. Leading 28-21 when Barrett was hurt, Ohio State finally got the cushion it needed when coach Urban Meyer went for it on fourth-and-1 from the Michigan 44-yard line with five minutes left, and Ezekiel Elliott broke free for a touchdown.

When linebacker Darron Lee returned a fumble caused by Joey Bosa 33 yards for another score a minute later, the victory was secured.

Until then, this was hardly the mismatch the oddsmakers expected.

A three-touchdown favorite against a Michigan team that needed a win to become bowl-eligible, Ohio State had every one of its punches answered by the Wolverines for two-and-a-half quarters.

Michigan's offense hardly looked like the one that had been stuck in neutral most of the season. A year ago, the Wolverines gouged Ohio State's defense with misdirection and screens. This was worse. Led by quarterback Devin Gardner, Michigan mostly bulled through the Buckeyes in a way that would have made Bo Schembechler proud.

Michigan used a total of 34 plays on three touchdown drives that knotted the score at 21.

At that point, Buckeyes senior defensive tackle

Quarterback J.T. Barrett turns the corner and scores a touchdown against Michigan in the third quarter. Barrett suffered a season-ending injury on his first play of the fourth quarter. (Kyle Robertson/Dispatch)

Michael Bennett called the defense together and ripped into it, with language hardly G-rated.

"I wanted to bring it to the forefront and eliminate all confusion," Bennett said. "We were just getting beat (man vs. man), and we had to go out there and beat our man lined up across from us every play."

While Bennett was chewing out his teammates, the Buckeyes launched a 14-play, 81-yard drive to take a 28-21 lead. Ohio State's defense answered by getting its first three-and-out.

Then came Barrett's injury. On their next series, the Buckeyes faced the pivotal fourth-and-1 at the 44. Meyer turned to offensive line coach Ed Warinner and asked if his unit could convert if he went for it. The answer, not surprisingly, was yes.

"It was a simple inside zone that the offensive line did a (heck) of a job blocking," offensive coordinator Tom Herman said.

Elliott broke a tackle attempt near the line of scrimmage by linebacker Jake Ryan, ran through a gaping hole opened by tackle Taylor Decker and guard Billy Price, and was gone.

So were Michigan's upset hopes, making the game likely the final one for coach Brady Hoke. But he was more frustrated that Michigan (5-7, 3-5) won't be headed to a bowl game.

"It's disappointing for all of us," he said. "It stinks for a lot of reasons, No. 1 the expectations you have for yourself, that you haven't met them … as a program and a team."

The Buckeyes' goals remain in reach, though Barrett's injury casts a pall on their chances.

But a victory over Michigan, even an imperfect and costly one, is worth savoring.

"There was a saying that you can lose every game other than this one. I don't buy that, but that's the way we approached this game," said Meyer, the first Ohio State coach to win his first three Michigan games since Francis Schmidt in the 1930s. "For those who grew up in the state of Ohio, this is The Game.

"Our guys are going to enjoy this, but they know what's ahead of them." ■

Linebacker Darron Lee returns a fumble for a touchdown during the fourth quarter. (Jonathan Quilter/Dispatch)

Wide receiver Devin Smith eludes Michigan
defensive back Raymon Taylor to catch
a 50-yard pass in the third quarter of
the game against Ohio State's archrival.
(Eamon Queeney/Dispatch)

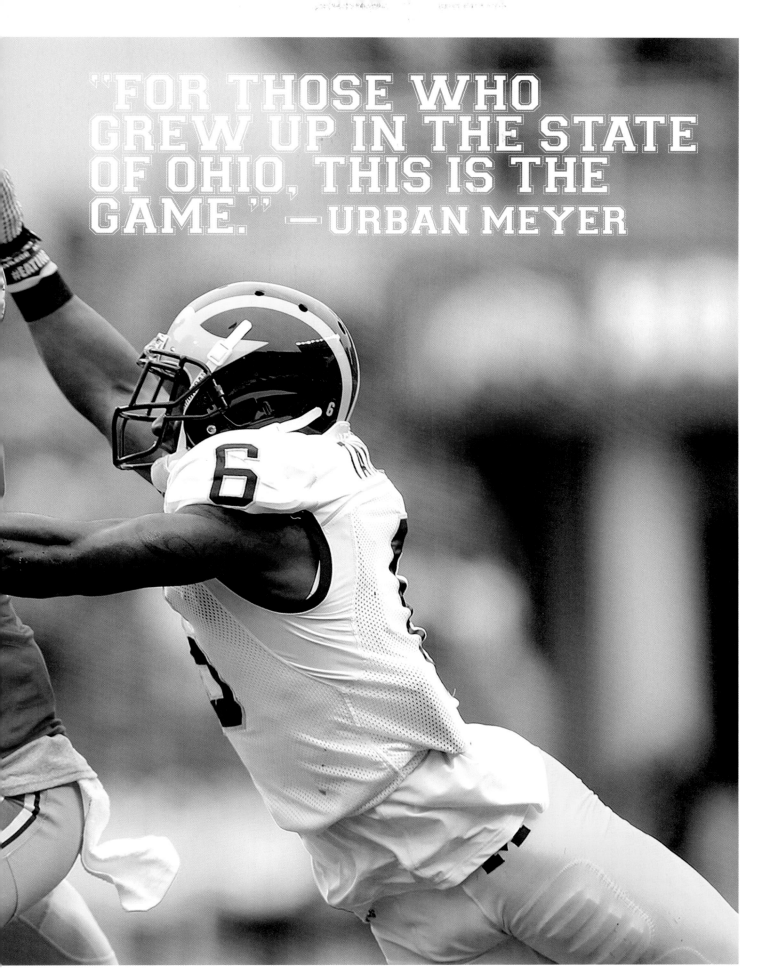

"FOR THOSE WHO GREW UP IN THE STATE OF OHIO, THIS IS THE GAME." —URBAN MEYER

#BUCKEYEPRIDE
Do it for
#53
#GOBUCKS
KOSTA!
ATHLETICO
PHYSICAL THERAPY
for every body.
#RIPKOS

MISSING OSU PLAYER FOUND DEAD

Football Players and Wrestlers Mourn Beloved Teammate
By Laura Arenschield and Bill Rabinowitz • December 1, 2014

Kosta Karageorge, a defensive tackle on the Ohio State football team, left his apartment early on Wednesday, just after he sent a cryptic text to his mother.

His family reported him missing and, throughout the holiday weekend, searchers combed Columbus looking for him.

Yesterday afternoon, a woman and her son were sifting through a dumpster near 6th and Courtland avenues when they found his body. The dumpster is around the corner from the apartment of Karageorge on E. 7th Avenue, close to the Short North Kroger.

The 22-year-old appeared to have killed himself, police said. A handgun was found near his body inside the dumpster.

The text he had sent on Wednesday said he was sorry "if I am an embarrassment, but these concussions have my head all f----- up."

Last night, about 150 students and friends gathered for a somber vigil on the Ohio State Oval in front of the library. There were stories, prayers and a performance of *Carmen Ohio*, the school alma mater, by a few members of the marching band.

Karageorge was remembered as a big guy with a heart to match who had a knack for raising the spirits of those who knew him.

"It's devastating," said Craig Thomas, 21, a senior who was on the OSU wrestling team with Karageorge and had known him since high school

Karageorge was planning to rejoin the Ohio State wrestling team after the football season ended.

The wrestling team practiced at 5 p.m. yesterday, about an hour after the news broke about the body being found. OSU wrestling coach Tom Ryan said the athletic department provided counselors for the team.

"There were a lot of tears," he said. "There was a lot of crying. That says something be-cause you know how men are. We don't cry in front of anybody and don't show weakness. But it was emotional."

Ryan said many on the team wondered if they could have done anything to prevent the tragedy.

"I've been doing this for 22 years. This is as tough as it gets," he said.

Columbus Police Sgt. Rich Weiner said investigators were able to identify Karageorge's body in part by his tattoos.

Weiner said police did not know if the handgun found inside the dumpster belonged to Karageorge.

"We are working to confirm that," Weiner said.

Karageorge's mother, Susan, told police that her son had had several concussions and had a few spells of being extremely confused, according to a police report. But Ryan said Karageorge didn't have any documented concussions as a wrestler.

Football players and those who were on OSU's wrestling team with Karageorge were among those who attended the vigil last night on the Oval.

Johnni DiJulius, 22, a senior and a wrestling teammate, told those gathered that Karageorge was the guy he would call "when I was broken down by the side of the highway and needed help."

Another wrestler, Josh Fox, 20, a junior, said he

A fan holds up a sign for the recently deceased Ohio State defensive lineman Kosta Karageorge before the Big Ten championship game. (Eamon Queeney/Dispatch)

remembered how Karageorge was loyal to his friends. He said his fallen teammate also had an admirable penchant for never giving up. "He would be down in a match but always found a way to get back up," Fox said. "We need to pray for the family. It's hard losing a son."

The Ohio State University Department of Athletics released a statement last evening saying the department was "shocked and saddened" to learn of Karageorge's death.

"Our thoughts and prayers are with the Karageorge family, and those who knew him, during this most difficult time," the department said.

Karageorge graduated from Thomas Worthington High School, where he was undefeated as a heavyweight wrestler his senior year until losing in the second round of the state tournament. He went on to wrestle for three years as a Buckeye after starting his college career at the University of Oklahoma. He spent a redshirt year there before transferring to Ohio State.

Then this August, Karageorge joined the Ohio State football team as a walk-on. He appeared in one game, against Penn State.

Karageorge did not show up for football practice on Wednesday and then on Thursday, something he never would have done, his worried family and friends told investigators.

Karageorge would have been one of 24 seniors recognized at Ohio Stadium on Saturday before their final home game against Michigan.

Instead, after the other seniors were introduced, a picture of Karageorge was shown on the stadium's video board, asking for help in finding him.

In postgame interviews on Saturday, his teammates expressed hope that he would be found safe.

During a teleconference for the Big Ten championship game, Buckeyes coach Urban Meyer was asked about Karageorge. He said that he had talked with someone close to the family but that there were no updates.

About an hour later, the 911 call came. ■

Dispatch Reporter Jim Woods contributed to this story.

Left: Urban Meyer discusses the death of player Kosta Karageorge at his weekly press conference at the Woody Hayes Athletic Center. (Eric Albrecht/Dispatch) Above: Ohio State players honored Karageorge, who wore No. 53, with a sticker on their helmets at the 2014 Big Ten championship game. (Kyle Robertson/Dispatch)

• RUNNING BACK •
EZEKIEL ELLIOTT

Overlooked and Unassuming, Elliott Has Developed into All-Around Back

By Bill Rabinowitz • December 6, 2014

Ezekiel Elliott is the other running back playing in the Big Ten championship game.

Unlike Wisconsin's Melvin Gordon, Elliott is not a 2,000-yard rusher or the Big Ten's offensive player of the year. The Ohio State sophomore won't be headed to New York as a Heisman Trophy finalist, as Gordon certainly will be.

Although Elliott hasn't received the accolades that Gordon has, his value to the Buckeyes can't be overstated and he could be more important than ever against the Badgers.

With Ohio State breaking in a new starting quarterback as Cardale Jones replaces the injured J.T. Barrett, it stands to reason that the Buckeyes will lean on Elliott's running.

Just as Barrett impressed this year with his even-tempered demeanor, Elliott has the same kind of workmanlike approach. He's not looking to make a statement; he's looking to do whatever he can to win.

"We approach every game the same way — be as prepared as possible, so when your number is called you can perform at an optimum capacity," Elliott said. "Our goal this week is to keep Cardale comfortable in the pocket, to make sure he doesn't feel pressure."

• • • • • • •

Ezekiel Elliott is named in honor of former New York Giants tight end Zeke Mowatt.

"Zeke Mowatt is my godfather," Elliott said. "He took my dad under his wing when he was in high school, and they've been really good friends ever since."

There's another story about his name, as well. Stacy Elliott said that his wife, Dawn, had a vision in which she saw wheels within a wheel.

"Me being a student of scripture," Stacy Elliott said, "I went to read the book of Ezekiel and saw that she described something very similar to what Ezekiel the prophet saw.

After rushing for 220 yards and two touchdowns in the Big Ten championship game, running back Ezekiel Elliott kisses the trophy. (Jonathan Quilter/Dispatch)

"After that, and because of my relationship with Ezekiel Mowatt, 'we' agreed (to name a son Ezekiel). I say that with quotation marks because Dawn was very adamant about naming her child."

Ezekiel got his athletic ability from both parents, who met as athletes at the University of Missouri. He was a linebacker. Dawn, who was a four-sport high-school athlete in Iowa, ran track.

But Stacy says that Ezekiel got his drive from his mom.

"His quality of attention to detail, that's his mother, 100 percent," Stacy said, laughing. "His work ethic — one speed — that's his mother, 100 percent."

Ezekiel was drawn to sports as soon as he could walk. Every photo of him as a boy, he said, has him holding a ball. If he didn't have a ball, he'd wad up socks.

"Ezekiel just was always very active," Dawn said. "It didn't matter what kind of ball it was. He was trying to throw it or play with it."

But even as a young athlete, he had a good heart.

"When he was about 10, he was playing little league football and we were playing against a team where one of their players — their best player — didn't have any cleats," Stacy said. "Ezekiel, without saying anything to anyone, went and got this little boy some of his cleats and gave it to him. He's a very caring young man."

The Elliotts made sure that sports were secondary to academics for Ezekiel and his younger sisters, Lailah and Aaliyah, as they grew up in Alton, Ill. Striving for perfection was imperative.

"That's definitely something my mom drilled into me when I was young," Ezekiel said. "Everything had to be perfect, (even needing to develop) perfect handwriting.

"I write like a girl," he added sheepishly, before providing a sample. (Impartial verdict: meticulous but not feminine.)

Elliott attended academically elite private schools in nearby St. Louis. He is a scholar-athlete at Ohio State and hopes to be admitted into the Fisher College of Business.

Elliott doesn't profess to lead the most dynamic life.

"All I do is go to practice, go to school, go home," he said. "I don't have time for much else, honestly."

He lives with star defensive end Joey Bosa.

"Joey's mom, Cheryl, said they reminded her of an old married couple," Dawn Elliott said.

Bosa is known for his shrug after sacks. Elliott has gained attention for tucking his jersey underneath his pads, a la former Buckeye Joey Galloway.

"I don't really like when people tackle me by grabbing my jersey, so I just tuck it up under my pads," Elliott said.

So it's a practical matter, not a fashion statement. That's fitting with Elliott's style.

He has run for 1,182 yards and 10 touchdowns this season, averaging 6.0 yards per carry. But coaches are at least as impressed by his versatility and work ethic.

Offensive coordinator Tom Herman said that Elliott practices harder than any other running back he has coached, and it reflects in his play.

"He can run inside," Herman said. "He can run outside. He can catch the ball. He can pass-protect.

"He does a lot of things for us. A lot of offenses don't have the luxury to have all those skill sets in one guy."

Elliott has done it with the full use of only one arm. He fractured a small bone in his left wrist during training camp and he required surgery. Even now, he can't hold the ball with his left hand and is only beginning to use it to stiff-arm tacklers.

But physical issues aren't the only ones that he and his teammates have had to overcome. The toughest has been the death of walk-on Kosta Karageorge last weekend. He and Elliott became friends this fall. Dawn Elliott said Karageorge was the first person her son was close to who has died.

"All year, we've been taking blows left and right," Elliott said. "We're a resilient team. The amount of things that we've gone through together has made us stronger and more close-knit. It's going to take a lot to get in our way. We've been through too much."

So even though Gordon will be the running back who will get most of the attention, the one on the other side will continue to do his job efficiently and quietly, for now.

"As he continues to grow," coach Urban Meyer said, "this whole country is going to hear about Zeke Elliott before it's all done." ■

Running back Ezekiel Elliott gallops for a chunk of his 97 total yards during Ohio State's 56-17 victory against Rutgers. (Fred Squillante/Dispatch)

BIG TEN CHAMPIONSHIP GAME

OHIO STATE 59, WISCONSIN 0
December 6, 2014 • Indianapolis, Indiana

COMMITTEE, IS THIS GOOD ENOUGH FOR YOU?

Buckeyes Romp Behind Backup QB Cardale Jones

By Bill Rabinowitz

Ohio State entered the Big Ten championship game last night having to win a two-pronged battle against Wisconsin.

The Buckeyes had to beat the favored Badgers, and quarterback Cardale Jones had to play well enough to show that Ohio State is worthy of consideration for one of the four spots in the inaugural College Football Playoff.

They couldn't have done it any better.

Jones was nearly flawless, and the Buckeyes' defense overwhelmed Wisconsin 59-0 at Lucas Oil Stadium to give Urban Meyer his first Big Ten championship.

The Buckeyes (12-1) had waited a year to avenge their defeat in last year's title game, and they had to overcome terrible adversity in the last week to do so.

Quarterback J.T. Barrett's fractured ankle against Michigan caused the Buckeyes to turn to Jones for his starting debut, and then the team was stunned by the death of walk-on defensive tackle Kosta Karageorge.

Then there was the challenge of facing Wisconsin (10-3) with its Heisman Trophy candidate, running back Melvin Gordon, and its defense, which ranked second nationally.

But it was no contest. Jones, who was named the game's most valuable player, showed no jitters and looked in complete command from the start. He completed 12 of 17 passes for 257 yards and three touchdowns, all to senior receiver Devin Smith.

"I was confident, but my teammates and coaches took my confidence to a whole other level that I've never felt before," Jones said.

Ezekiel Elliott ran 20 times for 220 yards and two scores, including an 81-yard run up the middle on which he was untouched.

The defense was just as impressive. It was air-tight against Gordon. The junior, who entered the game averaging 188 yards per game and 8.0 per carry, was held to 76 yards in 26 carries. His longest gain against Ohio State was 13 yards.

"Any shutout is great, but the way we went about it, you have to give the credit to the guys up front," defensive coordinator Luke Fickell said. "When they can't block the edge, it makes it a lot more difficult."

Gordon's ineffectiveness forced the Badgers to the air, for which they're ill-suited. Doran Grant (twice) and Vonn Bell intercepted Joel Stave, who completed only 17 of 43 passes for 187 yards.

The Buckeyes wasted no time seizing control. Michael Thomas made a diving catch of Jones' pass

Quarterback Cardale Jones, who completed 12 of 17 passes for 257 yards and three touchdowns during his first career start, throws during the second quarter. (Kyle Robertson/Dispatch)

Devin Smith (9) hauls in a 39-yard reception in the first quarter. (Eamon Queeney/Dispatch)

on the game's first snap. Five plays later, Jones threw a 39-yard touchdown to Smith, who warded off Wisconsin cornerback Sojourn Shelton.

The Buckeyes took a 14-0 lead on Elliott's touchdown run and settled for a field goal after Bell's interception.

Then Jones threw to Smith for a 44-yard touchdown to make it 24-0 early in the second quarter. Jones completed three straight passes on Ohio State's next drive to set up a 14-yard touchdown run by Elliott.

The Buckeyes made it 38-0 with 36 seconds left in the half. Defensive tackle Michael Bennett, wearing No. 53 in honor of Karageorge, poked the ball free from Gordon. Defensive end Joey Bosa picked up the ball at the 4 and scored.

As if there was any doubt about the outcome, the Buckeyes scored on their first drive of the second half when Smith made a leaping catch in tight coverage for a 42-yard score.

The only drama after that was whether the Buckeyes could get the shutout. Wisconsin did not advance past the Ohio State 27-yard line until the final play of the game.

Now, the Buckeyes must wait to learn their postseason fate. Alabama and Oregon are locks after winning their conference title games. Reigning national champion Florida State would seem to be after it again survived an upset bid, this time in the ACC title game.

But the Big 12, which has No. 3 TCU and No. 6 Baylor, doesn't have a championship game. Both won yesterday, but Ohio State's win was the most impressive.

"We deserve to be in," athletic director Gene Smith said. "We're a championship team. We have a conference championship game and we went through our regular-season gantlet and had the opportunity to come here and play another game. To me, that's an edge." ■

Running back Ezekiel Elliott, who had 220 of Ohio State's 301 rushing yards, celebrates his 14-yard touchdown in the second quarter. (Jonathan Quilter/ Dispatch)

Cornerback Doran Grant (12) and linebacker Curtis Grant, right, raise the Stagg Championship Trophy after Ohio State beat Wisconsin 59-0 in the 2014 Big Ten championship game. (Kyle Robertson/Dispatch)

(Kyle Robertson/Dispatch)